The Daily Reader
for Contemplative Living

The
Daily Reader for
Contemplative Living

Excerpts from the Works of
Father Thomas Keating, O.C.S.O.,
Sacred Scripture, and Other Spiritual Writings

Compiled by

S. STEPHANIE IACHETTA

BLOOMSBURY
NEW YORK · LONDON · NEW DELHI · SYDNEY

A Continuum Book
Bloomsbury Publishing Plc
50 Bedford Square
London WC1B 3DP

www.bloomsbury.com

Bloomsbury Publishing, London, New Delhi, New York and Sydney

First published 2009

A CIP record for this book is available from the Library of Congress

Keating, Thomas
The daily reader for contemplative living: excerpts from the works of
Thomas Keating, O.C.S.O.: sacred Scripture, and other spiritual writing/complied by
S. Stephanie Iachetta.
p. cm.
Includes index.
ISBN: 0-8264-1515-6 (alk. paper)
ISBN-13: 978-0-8264-3354-1
1. Devotional calenders–Catholic Church. I. Iachetta, S. Stephanie. II. Title.
BV4810.K43 2003
242'.2–dc21   2003003520

ISBN: 978-0-8264-3354-1

10 9 8 7 6 5 4 3

Printed and bound in the U.S.A. by Thomson-Shore Inc., Dexter, Michigan

And the Word was made flesh,
and dwelt among us....

John 1:14 KJV

Contents

Foreword

Some books, like some people, can be pronounced "wonderful" after only a brief encounter; more meetings simply reinforce our initial judgment. This is that sort of book, an ideal vade mecum for those who desire to retrieve the wonderfulness so often obscured by the distracting demands of our ordinary routines, the sheer dailiness of our daily lives that dulls our spiritual sensitivities. Here then is the wake-up call we need to "seize the day" once again by attending to the promptings within our hearts and allowing the most gentle of companions to accompany us through it.

The book's structure is both simple and elegant. Each day's text begins with a line of prayer, a "prayer sentence" that acts as both a theme and an invitation. Each closes with an appropriate, longer citation from Scripture that is a Biblically based recapitulation of the theme. In between lies a short reflection to inspire meditation, each an excerpt from the writings of the Cistercian monk, Father Thomas Keating, a noted retreat master and founder of the Centering Prayer Movement and of Contemplative Outreach. Father Keating's comments will reassure those who are a bit frightened by the heady altitudes erroneously associated with contemplative prayer; and his sensible suggestions, firmly rooted in the rich tradition of the great Catholic mystics like Teresa of Avila and John of the Cross, will remind us that prayer is not work, but an attentive waiting followed by surrender.

So the words in this book are few and meant merely to be supportive. They have been specifically chosen to encourage a spiritual silence and to create an interior space in which the voice of the Spirit might whisper and find echo within the innermost chambers of one's self. Such words make for a wonderful book.

GEORGE W. HUNT, S.J.

Acknowledgments

My deepest gratitude and thanks go to:

Father Thomas Keating and The Continuum Publishing Company for their support of my idea and permission to use Father Keating's materials and agreement to publish the finished project.

My family for their confidence in me and their unselfish sharing of their talents. This includes my fiction- and newspaper-writer husband, Michael, for his deep love, affection, and encouragement; my son and scholar Michael for his attention to detail and insights into Scripture; my daughters, Stephanie and Martha, for their editing expertise; and my son Charles for his technical assistance.

My friend and mentor Grace Shaw for her guidance emanating from her successful career as an editor for a major New York publishing company. Her advice and encouragement were crucial, especially in the early doubt-filled days.

My "sisters" on this contemplative journey, Diane Harkin and Jane Byrne who prayed for me "without ceasing."

My friends in Contemplative Outreach for their love, prayers, and insights into spiritual writers and Scripture.

Marianne Lacy and the late Father Peter McCall and other faith-healing members of the House of Peace who loved me and prayed with me for health of body, mind, and spirit and for the successful completion of this book.

Sister Winifred Danowitz, an Ursuline nun from the College of New Rochelle, mentor and long-time friend, whose common-sense approach to life and unwavering support and belief in me helped motivate me in moments of doubt.

My friend and mentor Ann Clemente for financial assistance during the early formative stage of the project.

For the contemplative living programs made available by Cathy McCarthy and Contemplative Outreach staff at St. Andrews Retreat House in Walden, New York, which gave direction to my search for a closer relationship with God.

And most of all, I am grateful to God for planning it all!

Introduction

Like many of you, I lead a full active life, seek a closer relationship with God, and am committed to a contemplative lifestyle. In addition to my two daily periods of Centering Prayer, I often found myself wishing for easily accessible written spiritual nourishment to complement that practice.

The idea of compiling a daily reader grew out of this desire. I wanted to combine the richness of a contemplative anthology with the convenience of a compact reader — small enough to fit in a purse, briefcase, or beside one's bed.

The Daily Reader for Contemplative Living ties together thematically three contemplative living prayer practices: an "active prayer," a reading from a spiritual writer, and a reading from Sacred Scripture. The brief introductory "prayer sentences" (active prayers) are either from Scripture, traditional prayers of the church, quotes from well-known spiritual writers, or from my own personal experience. All of the short meditations here (spiritual readings) are excerpts from one of the works of Father Thomas Keating, a pioneering Cistercian monk, dedicated to the spread of the ecumenical contemplative prayer movement. Each day's entry closes with a selection from the Bible. I draw the Scripture from both Christian and Judaic texts. Sacred Scripture comes last to give the reader the opportunity to move easily into the prayer practice of *Lectio Divina* — reflecting on Scripture and finally resting with God's Word.

Each month features excerpts from one of Keating's works. For example, January focuses on excerpts from his book *Open Mind, Open Heart*, and September offers excerpts from his audiotape *Who Is God?* The appendix contains "The Essentials of the Centering Prayer Method," reprinted from *Open Mind, Open Heart*. Indexes include biblical references, subjects, quotations, and active prayer sentences.

Who exactly is Thomas Keating and why would anyone be interested in what he has to say?

Thomas Keating, Order of Cistercians Strict Observance (O.C.S.O.), is a Trappist monk and former abbot of St. Joseph's Abbey in Spencer, Massachusetts. He currently resides at St. Benedict's Monastery in Snowmass, Colorado, where he gives intensive ten-day retreats on Centering Prayer. Keating is a founder of the Centering Prayer Movement and of Contemplative Outreach — a worldwide spiritual network of individuals and small faith communities that supports the practice of Centering Prayer. Keating has addressed international audiences, spoken at the Harvard Divinity School, and conducted retreats worldwide. He is regarded as a pioneer in the widespread renewal of the contemplative dimension of the Gospel.

In his book *Open Mind, Open Heart*, Father Keating writes: "Christian Contemplative Prayer is the opening of mind and heart — our whole being — to God, the Ultimate Mystery, beyond thoughts, words and emotions, whom we know by faith is within us, closer than breathing, thinking, feeling and choosing; even closer than consciousness itself. The root of all prayer is interior silence."

Father Keating advocates Centering Prayer as a method of prayer that prepares one to receive the gift of Contemplative Prayer. He describes Centering Prayer as both a relationship and a discipline — a relationship of communion with God and a discipline to facilitate this relationship. Centering Prayer makes use of a "sacred word" that is designed to lead into silence and is a symbol of one's intention to consent to God's presence and action within. The individual selects a sacred word — one to two syllables, e.g., *Jesus, God, Love, Joy* — and introduces it on the level of the imagination. Says Keating, "Gently place it in your awareness each time you recognize you are thinking about some other thought." Keating does not discourage thoughts. He does *not* advocate a "blank" mind. He considers both silence and thoughts an integral part of the purification process (the Divine Therapy) and recommends *detachment from* rather than elimination of thoughts.

In *Open Mind, Open Heart* Father Keating suggests several prayer practices that extend the contemplative effects of Centering Prayer into one's day. The active prayer is one of many practices that expresses our intention to consent to God's presence and action within. These brief, five-to-nine-syllable prayers are simple enough to easily remember and repeat to one's self throughout the day. For example, this prayer can be an aspiration drawn from Scripture, such as *My Lord and my God* or a counsel from Abba Isaac, one of the Desert Fathers belonging to a fourth-century lay contemplative movement, such as *God, come to my assistance.* I enjoy personalizing my active prayer. When I was compiling this book, I chanted *Lover, Creator, Healer, shine through.* While I was remodeling my kitchen, it became *Lord, give me courage to make changes.* By repeating a positive aspiration throughout the day, it gradually works its way into the subconscious and affirms one's life and counteracts any disturbing thoughts that surface as automatic responses to the vagaries of life.

Other contemplative prayer practices that extend the effects of Centering Prayer into the day include *Lectio Divina* and spiritual reading. In them you may find, as did Saint Thérèse of Lisieux, solid and very pure nourishment. From the contemplative viewpoint, one reads for *formation* rather than *information* and responds with one's heart and spirit rather than with reason.

Because these prayer practices support a contemplative lifestyle, they make up the core of *The Daily Reader for Contemplative Living*.

List of Abbreviations

Books by Father Thomas Keating

The Continuum International Publishing Group,
15 East 26th Street, New York, NY 10010

OM	*Open Mind, Open Heart*
CF	*Crisis of Faith, Crisis of Love*
IL	*Invitation to Love*
MC	*The Mystery of Christ*
BP	*The Better Part*

The Crossroad Publishing Company,
481 Eighth Avenue, Suite 1550, New York, NY 10001

AW	*Awakenings*
HW	*The Heart of the World*
IG	*Intimacy with God*

Lantern Books, One Union Square West, Suite 201,
New York, NY 10003

FG	*Fruits and Gifts of the Spirit*

Paulist Press, 997 Macarthur Boulevard,
Mahwah, NJ 07430

HC	*The Human Condition*

Keating Audiotape
Text from the audiotape was transcribed by the author of
The Daily Reader for Contemplative Living from a Thomas
Keating audiotape of a meeting called "Contemplative
Prayer in the Twenty-first Century" held September 30,
2000, at the Holiday Inn at O'Hare Airport.

WG   Who Is God?

THE HOLY BIBLE

KJV	King James Version
NAB	New American Bible
NASB	New American Standard Bible
NIV	New International Version
NKJV	New King James Version
NJB	The New Jerusalem Bible
NRSV	New Revised Standard Version
NLT	New Living Translation
TCLB	The Catholic Living Bible
THS	The Holy Scriptures

· *January 1* ·

Contemplative Prayer

The Lord let his face shine upon you....
Numbers 6:25 NAB

Contemplative prayer is a process of interior transformation, a conversation initiated by God and leading, if we consent, to divine union. One's way of seeing reality changes in this process. A restructuring of consciousness takes place which empowers one to perceive, relate and respond with increasing sensitivity to the divine presence in, through, and beyond everything that exists. (*OM*, 4)

Numbers 6:24–26 NAB

The Lord bless you and keep you!
The Lord let his face shine upon you,
  and be gracious to you!
The Lord look upon you kindly and give you peace!

· *January 2* ·

Our Spiritual Journey

And over all these put on love. . . .
Colossians 3:14 NAB

Dedication to God is developed by commitment to one's spiritual practices for God's sake. Service to others is the outgoing movement of the heart prompted by compassion. It neutralizes the deep-rooted tendency to become preoccupied with our own spiritual journey and how we are doing. The habit of service to others is developed by trying to please God in what we do and by exercising compassion for others, beginning with those with whom we live. To accept everyone unconditionally is to fulfill the commandment to "love your neighbor as yourself" (Mark 12:31). It is a practical way of bearing one another's burdens (Galatians 6:2). Refusing to judge even in the face of persecution is to fulfill the commandment to love one another "as I have loved you" (John 13:34) and to lay down one's life for one's friends (John 15:13). *(OM, 15–16)*

Colossians 3:12–14 NAB

Put on then, as God's chosen ones, holy and beloved, heartfelt compassion, kindness, humility, gentleness, and patience, bearing with one another and forgiving one another, if one has a grievance against another; as the Lord has forgiven you, so must you also do. And over all these put on love. . . .

· *January 3* ·

Only a Radiance of His Presence

[He dwells] in inaccessible light....
1 Timothy 6:16 NJB

Anything that we perceive of God can only be a radiance of His presence and not God as He is Himself. When the divine light strikes the human mind, it breaks down into many aspects just as a ray of ordinary light, when it strikes a prism, breaks down into the varied colors of the spectrum. There is nothing wrong with distinguishing different aspects of the Ultimate Mystery, but it would be a mistake to identify them with the inaccessible Light. The attraction to let go of spiritual consolation in order to let God act with complete freedom is the persistent attraction of the Spirit. The more one lets go, the stronger the presence of the Spirit becomes. The Ultimate Mystery becomes the Ultimate Presence. (*OM*, 17)

1 Timothy 6:16 NASB

He who is the blessed and only Sovereign, the King of kings and Lord of lords, who alone possesses immortality and dwells in unapproachable light, whom no man has seen or can see. To Him be honor and eternal dominion! Amen.

· January 4 ·

Communication from the Spirit of God

Where can I go from your Spirit....
Psalm 139:7 NIV

The Spirit speaks to our conscience through scripture and through the events of daily life. Reflection on these two sources of personal encounter and the dismantling of the emotional programming of the past prepare the psyche to listen at more refined levels of attention. The Spirit then begins to address our conscience from that deep source within us which is our true Self. This is contemplation properly so-called. (*OM*, 17)

Psalm 139:7–10 NIV

Where can I go from your Spirit?
Where can I flee from your presence?
If I go up to the heavens, you are there;
if I make my bed in the depths, you are there.
If I rise on the wings of the dawn,
if I settle on the far side of the sea,
even there your hand will guide me,
your right hand will hold me fast.

· January 5 ·

Opening and Surrendering to God's Presence Within

Be still before the LORD....
Psalm 37:7 NRSV

The spiritual journey does not require going anywhere because God is already with us and in us. It is a question of allowing our ordinary thoughts to recede into the background and to float along the river of consciousness without our noticing them, while we direct our attention toward the river on which they are floating. We are like someone sitting on the bank of a river and watching the boats go by. If we stay on the bank, with our attention on the river rather than on the boats, the capacity to disregard thoughts as they go by will develop, and a deeper kind of attention will emerge. (*OM*, 35)

Psalm 37:7 NRSV

Be still before the LORD,
and wait patiently for him....

· *January 6* ·

Sacred Word as Symbol

A short prayer pierces the heavens.
The Cloud of Unknowing

The sacred word is a sign or arrow pointing in the direction you want to take. It is a way of renewing your intention to open yourself to God and to accept Him as He is. While this does not prevent anyone from praying in other forms at other times, the period of centering prayer is not the time to pray specifically for others. By opening yourself to God, you are implicitly praying for everyone past, present, and future. You are embracing the whole of creation. You are accepting all reality, beginning with God and with that part of your own reality of which you may not be generally aware, namely, the spiritual level of your being. (*OM*, 43)

Isaiah 30:21 NIV

Whether you turn to the right or to the left,
your ears will hear a voice behind you, saying,
"This is the way; walk in it."

· *January 7* ·

Intimacy with God

I am the vine, you are the branches....
John 15:5 NASB

The chief thing that separates us from God is the thought that we are separated from Him.... We fail to believe that we are always with God and that He is part of every reality. The present moment, every object we see, our inmost nature are all rooted in Him. But we hesitate to believe this until personal experience gives us the confidence to believe in it. This involves the gradual development of intimacy with God. God constantly speaks to us through each other as well as from within. The interior experience of God's presence activates our capacity to perceive Him in everything else — in people, in events, in nature. (*OM*, 44)

Romans 8:38–39 NASB

For I am convinced that neither death, nor life, nor angels, nor principalities, nor things present, nor things to come, nor powers, nor height, nor depth, nor any other created thing, will be able to separate us from the love of God, which is in Christ Jesus our Lord.

· January 8 ·

Inner Transformation

I am the LORD who heals you.
Exodus 15:26 NLT

In contemplative prayer the Spirit places us in a position where we are at rest and disinclined to fight. By his secret anointings the Spirit heals the wounds of our fragile human nature at a level beyond our psychological perception, just as a person who is anesthetized has no idea of how the operation is going until after it is over. Interior silence is the perfect seedbed for divine love to take root. In the Gospel the Lord speaks about a mustard seed as a symbol of divine love. It is the smallest of all seeds, but it has an enormous capacity for growth. Divine love has the power to grow and to transform us. The purpose of contemplative prayer is to facilitate the process of inner transformation. (*OM*, 45)

Jeremiah 30:17 NIV

"I will restore you to health and heal your wounds," declares the LORD....

· *January 9* ·

God's First Language Is Silence

My sheep hear My voice. . . .
John 10:27 NASB

There are all kinds of ways in which God speaks to us —
through our thoughts or any one of our faculties. But
keep in mind that God's first language is silence. Prepare
yourself for silence in this prayer, and if other things
happen, that is His problem, not yours. As soon as you
make it your problem, you tend to desire something that
is other than God. Pure faith will bring you closer to
God than anything else. To be attached to an experience
of God is not God; it is a thought. The time of centering
prayer is the time to let go of all thoughts, even the best
of thoughts. If they are really good, they will come back
later. (*OM*, 57)

John 10:27 NASB

My sheep hear My voice, and I know them, and they
follow Me. . . .

· *January 10* ·

Bring Christ into the World

Immanuel ... means, "God with us."
Matthew 1:23 NIV

What is the great thing that Our Lady has done for us? She brought the Word of God into the world, or rather let Him come into the world through her. It is not so much what we do but what we *are* that allows Christ to live in the world. When the presence of God emerges from our inmost being into our faculties, whether we walk down the street or drink a cup of soup, divine life is pouring into the world. The effectiveness of every action depends on the source from which it springs. If it is coming out of the false self, it is severely limited. If it is coming out of a person who is immersed in God, it is extremely effective. The contemplative state, like the vocation of Our Lady, brings Christ into the world. (*OM*, 62–63)

Matthew 1:22–23 NIV

All this took place to fulfill what the Lord had said through the prophet: "The virgin will be with child and will give birth to a son, and they will call him Immanuel" — which means, "God with us."

· January 11 ·

A Strengthening and Affirming Experience

Jesus the Christ heals you.
Acts 9:34 NKJV

Interior silence is one of the most strengthening and affirming of human experiences. There is nothing more affirming, in fact, than the experience of God's presence. That revelation says as nothing else can, "You are a good person. I created you and I love you." Divine love brings us into being in the fullest sense of the word. It heals the negative feelings we have about ourselves. (*OM*, 66)

Acts 3:19 NKJV

Times of refreshing...come from the presence of the Lord....

· January 12 ·

Our Relationship with God

May...God...comfort and strengthen your hearts....
2 Thessalonians 2:16–17 NASB

The alternations in our relationship with God are not
unlike the presence or absence of someone we greatly
love. In the *Song of Solomon,* God is depicted as pursuing
the soul as His beloved. The fathers of the Church had
a fondness for this particular verse: "O that his left hand
were under my head and that his right hand embraced
me" (Song of Solomon 2:6). According to their inter-
pretation, God embraces us with both arms. With the
left He humbles and corrects us; with the right He lifts
us up and consoles us with the assurance of being loved
by Him. If you want to be fully embraced by the Lord,
you have to accept both arms: the one that allows suffering for the sake of purification and the one that brings
the joy of union. When you feel physical pain or when
psychological struggles are persecuting you, you should
think that God is hugging you extra tightly. Trials are
an expression of His Love, not of rejection. (*OM,* 76)

Song of Songs 2:6 THS

Let his left hand be under my head,
And his right hand embrace me.

· January 13 ·

Trust in the Lord

In God do I trust....
Psalm 56:12 THS

The more confidence you have in God, the more you can face the truth about yourself. You can only face up to who you really are in the presence of someone you trust. If you trust God, you know that no matter what you have done or not done, He is going to go on loving you. As a matter of fact, He always knew the dark side of your character and He is now letting you in on the secret like a friend confiding to a friend. Insights of self-knowledge, instead of upsetting you, bring a sense of freedom. They lead you to the point where you can ask yourself, "Why think of myself at all?" Then you have the freedom to think how wonderful God is and you care little what happens to you. (*OM*, 90)

John 8:31–32 NJB

If you make my word your home you will indeed be my disciples; you will come to know the truth, and the truth will set you free.

· January 14 ·

Surrender of the False Self

The Spirit gives birth to spirit.
John 3:6 NIV

When you are in perfect prayer, the Spirit is praying in you. The surrender of the false self to God is death to the false self. This is the experience that Jesus was trying to explain to Nicodemus when he said, "You have to be reborn" (John 3:3). One has to die before one can be reborn. Nicodemus replied, "How can someone go back into the womb?" Jesus continued, "You do not understand what I am talking about. I am talking about the Spirit and I am speaking spiritually. The wind blows where it will, and you do not know where it is coming from or where it is going. So it is with everyone who is born of the Spirit." In other words, to be moved by the Spirit is an entirely new way of being in the world. (*OM*, 91)

John 3:3 NIV

In reply Jesus declared, "I tell you the truth, no one can see the kingdom of God unless he is born again."

· January 15 ·

Christ-Centered Relationships

Soul of Christ, sanctify me.
Anima Christi

The insight into Christ dwelling in every other person enables one to express charity toward others with
greater spontaneity. Instead of seeing only someone's
personality, race, nationality, gender, status, or characteristics (which you like or do not like), you see what
is deepest — one's union or potential union with Christ.
You also perceive everyone's desperate need of help. The
transcendent potential of most people is still waiting to
be realized, and this awakens a great sense of compassion. This Christ-centered love takes us out of ourselves
and brings our newly found sense of independence into
relationships that are not based on dependency, as many
relationships tend to be, but that are based on Christ as
their center. It enables one to work for others with great
liberty of spirit because one is no longer seeking one's
own ego-centered goals but responding to reality as it
is. (*OM*, 103)

Galatians 3:28 NLT

Christians — you are one in Christ Jesus.

· January 16 ·

Centering Prayer and the Sacred Word

Closer my God to thee.
Traditional Hymn

The sacred word is a simple thought that you are thinking at ever deepening levels of perception.... The word on your lips is exterior and has no part in this form of prayer. The thought in your imagination is interior; the word as an impulse of your will is more interior still. Only when you pass beyond the word into pure awareness is the process of interiorization complete. That is what Mary of Bethany was doing at the feet of Jesus. She was going beyond the words she was hearing to the Person who was speaking and entering into union with Him. This is what we are doing as we sit in centering prayer interiorizing the sacred word. We are going beyond the sacred word into union with that to which it points — the Ultimate Mystery, the Presence of God, beyond any perception that we can form of Him. (*OM*, 111)

Ephesians 3:12 NLT

Because of Christ and our faith in him, we can now come fearlessly into God's presence, assured of his glad welcome.

· January 17 ·

Interior Purification

I will heal my people....
Jeremiah 33:6 NIV

Any form of meditation or prayer that transcends thinking sets off the dynamic of interior purification. This dynamic is God's school of psychotherapy. It enables the organism to release deep rooted tension in the form of thoughts.... Through this process, the undigested psychological material of a lifetime is gradually evacuated, the emotional investment of early childhood in programs for happiness based on instinctual drives is dismantled, and the false self gives way to the true self. Once you grasp the fact that thoughts are not only inevitable, but an integral part of the process of healing and growth initiated by God, you are able to take a positive view of them. Instead of looking upon them as painful distractions, you see them in a broader perspective that includes both interior silence and thoughts — thoughts that you do not want, but which, are just as valuable for the purpose of purification, as moments of profound tranquility. (*OM*, 113)

Jeremiah 33:6 NIV

I will heal my people and will let them enjoy abundant peace and security.

· January 18 ·

Long-Range Fruits of Centering Prayer

Live in ... [and] follow the Spirit.
Galatians 5:25 NAB

Don't judge centering prayer on the basis of how many thoughts come or how much peace you enjoy. The only way to judge this prayer is by its long-range fruits: whether in daily life you enjoy greater peace, humility and charity. Having come to deep interior silence, you begin to relate to others beyond the superficial aspects of social status, race, nationality, religion, and personal characteristics. (*OM*, 114)

Galatians 5:22–23, 25 NAB

The fruit of the Spirit is love, joy, peace, patience, kindness, generosity, faithfulness, gentleness, self-control. ... If we live in the Spirit, let us also follow the Spirit.

· January 19 ·

Faith in the Divine Presence

One believes with the heart. . . .
Romans 10:10 NRSV

There are times in one's life when the divine action is very strong and hard to resist. There are also times when the Lord seems to forget about you. The main thing is to accept whatever comes, to adjust to what happens to whatever He gives you. By alternating the sense of His closeness and distance, God trains our faculties to accept the mystery of His Presence beyond any kind of sensible or conceptual experience. The divine Presence is very close and immediate, when we are doing the most ordinary actions. Faith should become so transparent that it does not need experience. But it takes a lot of experience to reach that point. (*OM*, 120)

Luke 8:50 NAB

[Jesus said,] "Do not be afraid; just have faith. . . ."

· January 20 ·

Becoming Fully Integrated

To live is Christ, and to die is gain.
Philippians 1:21 NKJV

As God brings the "new man" to life in interior silence, that is to say, the new *you*, with the world view that Christ shares with you in deep silence, His view of things becomes more important to you than your own. Then He asks you to live that new life in the circumstances of everyday life, in your daily routine, contradicted by noise, opposition, and anxieties. These seem to persecute you because you want to be alone to relish that silence. But it is important to allow oneself to be confronted by daily life. The alternation between deep silence and action gradually brings the two together. You become fully integrated, a contemplative and yet fully capable of action at the same time. You are Mary and Martha at once. (*OM*, 120)

Philippians 1:21, 23–24 NKJV

For to me, to live is Christ, and to die is gain.... For I am hard-pressed between the two, having a desire to depart and be with Christ, which is far better. Nevertheless to remain in the flesh is more needful for you.

· January 21 ·

Commitment to Centering Prayer

Teach me to do your will. . . .
Psalm 143:10 NJB

Centering prayer is the keystone of a comprehensive
commitment to the contemplative dimensions of the
Gospel. Two periods a day of twenty to thirty minutes —
one in the early morning and one halfway through the
day or in the early evening — maintain the reservoir of
interior silence at a high level at all times. . . . To find
time for a second period later in the day may require
special effort. If you have to be available to your family as soon as you walk in the door, you might center
during your lunch hour. Or you might stop on the way
home from work and center in a church or park. If it
is impossible to get a second period of prayer in, it is
important that you lengthen the first one. (*OM*, 123)

Psalm 143:8 NJB

Let dawn bring news of your faithful love,
for I place my trust in you;
show me the road I must travel
for you to relieve my heart.

· January 22 ·

Fundamental Goodness of Human Nature

Everything God created is good....
1 Timothy 4:4 NIV

The fundamental goodness of human nature, like the mystery of the Trinity, Grace, and the Incarnation, is an essential element of Christian faith. This basic core of goodness is capable of unlimited development; indeed, of becoming transformed into Christ and deified. ... Our basic core of goodness is our true Self. Its center of gravity is God. The acceptance of our basic goodness is a quantum leap in the spiritual journey.... God and our true Self are not separate. Though we are not God, God and our true Self are the same thing. (*OM*, 127)

Genesis 1:27 NRSV

So God created humankind in his image,
in the image of God he created them;
male and female he created them.

· *January 23* ·

Presence and Action of Christ in Our lives

My Presence will go with you....
Exodus 33:14 NKJV

Grace is the presence and action of Christ at every moment of our lives. The sacraments are ritual actions in which Christ is present in a special manner, confirming and sustaining the major commitments of our Christian life.... In Baptism, the false self is ritually put to death, the new self is born, and the victory over sin won by Jesus through his death and resurrection is placed at our disposal. Not our uniqueness as persons, but our sense of separation from God and from others is destroyed in the death-dealing and life-giving waters of Baptism.... The Eucharist is the celebration of life: the coming together of all the material elements of the cosmos, their emergence to consciousness in human persons and the transformation of human consciousness into Divine consciousness. It is the manifestation of the Divine in and through the Christian community. We receive the Eucharist in order to become the Eucharist. (*OM*, 128)

Exodus 33:14 NKJV

My Presence will go with you,
and I will give you rest.

· January 24 ·

The Way to Divine Love

Behold, I make all things new.
Revelation 21:5 NAB

Divine love is compassionate, tender, luminous, totally
self-giving, seeking no reward, unifying everything....
The experience of being loved by God enables us to
accept our false self as it is, and then to let go of it
and journey to our true Self. The inward journey to
our true Self is the way to divine love.... The growing
awareness of our true Self, along with the deep sense of
spiritual peace and joy which flow from this experience,
balances the psychic pain of the disintegrating and dying
of the false self. As the motivating power of the false
self diminishes, our true Self builds the *new self* with
the motivating force of divine love. (*OM*, 129)

Ephesians 3:17–19 NAB

[I pray] ... that you ... may have strength ... to know the
love of Christ that surpasses knowledge, so that you may
be filled with all the fullness of God.

· January 25 ·

Community of Faith

Body of Christ, save me.
Anima Christi

A community of faith offers the support of example, correction, and mutual concern in the spiritual journey. Above all, participating in the mystery of Christ through the celebration of the liturgy, Eucharist, and silent prayer binds the community in a common search for transformation and union with God. The presence of Christ is ministered to each other and becomes tangible in the community, especially when it is gathered for worship or engaged in some work of service to those in need. (*OM*, 130)

1 Corinthians 12:25–26 NLT

All the members [of the body of Christ] care for each other equally. If one part suffers, all the parts suffer with it, and if one part is honored, all the parts are glad.

· *January 26* ·

Become Fully Human

Thanks, Lord, for the gift of who I am.

The goal of genuine spiritual practice is not the rejection of the good things of the body, mind, or spirit, but the right use of them. No aspect of human nature or period of human life is to be rejected but integrated into each successive level of unfolding self-consciousness. In this way, the partial goodness proper to each stage of human development is preserved and only its limitations are left behind. The way to become divine is thus to become fully human. (*OM*, 131)

1 Corinthians 15:10 NJB

What I am now,
I am through the grace of God,
and the grace which was given to me
has not been wasted.

· January 27 ·

Transforming Power of Divine Love

Oh, what a wonderful God we have!
Romans 11:33 NLT

The disintegrating and dying of our false self is our participation in the passion and death of Jesus. The building of our *new self,* based on the transforming power of divine love, is our participation in his risen life.... In the beginning, emotional hang-ups are the chief obstacle to the growth of our *new self* because they put our freedom into a straight jacket. Later, because of the subtle satisfaction that springs from self-control, spiritual pride becomes the chief obstacle. And finally, reflection of self becomes the chief obstacle because this hinders the innocence of divine union.... Human effort depends on grace even as it invites it. Whatever degree of divine union we may reach bears no proportion to our effort. It is the sheer gift of divine love. (*OM,* 132)

Romans 11:35–36 NLT

And who could ever give him so much that he would have to pay it back? For everything comes from him; everything exists by his power and is intended for his glory. To him be glory evermore. Amen.

· January 28 ·

The Way

All the ways of the LORD are loving....
Psalm 25:10 NIV

Jesus did not teach a specific method of meditation or bodily discipline for quieting the imagination, memory, and emotions. We should choose a spiritual practice adapted to our particular temperament and natural disposition. We must also be willing to dispense with it when called by the Spirit to surrender to his direct guidance. The Spirit is above every method or practice. To follow his inspiration is the sure path to perfect freedom.... What Jesus proposed to his disciples as the Way is his own example: the forgiveness of everything and everyone and the service of others in their needs. "Love one another as I have loved you." (*OM*, 132)

John 15:12 NJB

This is my commandment:
love one another,
as I have loved you.

· January 29 ·

Weekly Support Group

Comfort and encourage each other....
1 Thessalonians 4:18 NLT

While centering prayer is done privately most of the time, a weekly sharing of the experience in a small group (up to fifteen) has proven to be very supportive, as well as a means of continuing education. The weekly meeting also serves as a means of accountability. Just knowing that one's support group is meeting together each week is an enormous encouragement to keep going, or an invitation to return to the practice of centering prayer if circumstances ... have prevented one from carrying out one's commitment to daily practice for a time. By sharing the experience of centering prayer with others, one's own discernment of the ups and downs of the practice is sharpened. The group serves as a source of encouragement and can normally solve problems that might arise regarding the method. The collective discernment of the group tends to be well balanced. (*OM*, 135)

Psalm 32:8 NLT

The LORD says,
"I will guide you along the best pathway for your life.
I will advise you and watch over you...."

· *January 30* ·

Ultimate Mystery

God, you are my God, I pine for you....
Psalm 63:1 NJB

The root of prayer is interior silence. We may think of prayer as thoughts or feelings expressed in words. But this is only one expression. Deep prayer is the laying aside of thoughts. It is the opening of mind and heart, body and feelings — our whole being — to God, the Ultimate Mystery, beyond words, thoughts, and emotions. We do not resist them or suppress them. We accept them as they are and go beyond them, not by effort, but by letting them all go by. We open our awareness to the Ultimate Mystery whom we know by faith is within us, closer than breathing, closer than thinking, closer than choosing — closer than consciousness itself. The Ultimate Mystery is the ground in which our being is rooted, the Source from whom our life emerges at every moment. (*OM*, 136)

Psalm 63:1 NJB

God, you are my God, I pine for you;
my heart thirsts for you,
my body longs for you,
as a land parched, dreary and waterless.

· *January 31* ·

Presence to Presence

We have the mind of Christ.
1 Corinthians 2:16 NAB

We surrender to the attraction of interior silence, tranquility, and peace. We do not try to feel anything, reflect about anything. Without effort, without trying, we sink into this Presence, letting everything else go. Let love alone speak: the simple desire to be one with the Presence, to forget self, and to rest in the Ultimate Mystery. This Presence is immense, yet so humble; awe-inspiring, yet so gentle; limitless, yet so intimate, tender and personal. I *know* that I am *known*. . . . We wait patiently; in silence, openness, and quiet attentiveness; motionless within and without. We surrender to the attraction to be still, to be loved, just to *be*. (*OM*, 137)

1 Corinthians 2:9–10 NAB

As it is written:
"What eye has not seen, and ear has not heard,
 and what has not entered the human heart,
 what God has prepared for those who love him,"
this God has revealed to us through the Spirit.

· *February 1* ·

The Purgative Way

Do everything without complaining....
Philippians 2:14 NIV

The family of Bethany is a household of persons at various stages of the spiritual life.... [Martha] exemplifies "good souls" at the beginning of the spiritual journey when they have the best intentions to serve God.... She is converted on the conscious level ... but not converted on the unconscious level of her motivation.... She is in the first stage of the spiritual journey — the Purgative Way. The Purgative Way consists in becoming aware of how our unconscious needs affect ordinary daily life including our service of God. It is unsettling for us to realize that, mixed in with our good intentions, are ... infantile attitudes.... [Martha] ... is active in the service of God but her activity is not contemplative service. She is working for herself. No doubt she thinks she is working solely for God, but in fact her motivation is mixed. (*BP,* 15–18)

Luke 10:40 NAB

Martha, burdened with much serving, came to him and said, "Lord, do you not care that my sister has left me by myself to do the serving? Tell her to help me."

· *February 2* ·

Word of Wisdom for Martha

Motives are weighed by the LORD.
Proverbs 16:2 NIV

The thrust of Jesus' initial teaching in the Gospel is the challenge to *grow up!* Our drive to obtain the symbols in an environment of security and survival, affection and esteem, and power and control is doomed to frustration. Martha virtually says to Jesus, "You had better get that sister of mine to help me if you want something to eat!" Jesus replies, "Martha!" We can almost feel the gentle tone of rebuke in Jesus' voice, "Martha. You are troubled about many things, but only one thing is necessary. Mary has chosen the better part and it will not be taken away from her." That was Jesus' word of wisdom for Martha. A word of wisdom is not necessarily a rebuke. It is simply a statement of fact. There is nothing wrong with Martha's activity. It is her motivation that is defective. In Christianity, motivation is everything. (*BP,* 18)

Luke 10:41–42 NAB

"Martha, Martha, you are anxious and worried about many things. There is need of only one thing. Mary has chosen the better part and it will not be taken from her."

· *February 3* ·

The Illuminative Level

Be still, and know that I am God....
Psalm 46:10 KJV

Let us now take a look at Mary's activity, or rather, her lack of activity. She is sitting at the feet of Jesus listening to his words. Her whole attention is focused on the Master. She is listening at a level much deeper than her ears can hear. It is the kind of listening that takes place when our spiritual faculties begin to vibrate to the divine life present in Christ. One who hears the word of God on this level keeps it.... Mary is entering into the Illuminative level. In this state, words and reasoning give way to intuition and the direct transmission of Jesus' divine presence. Mary can hear at this level because of the increase of her faith. Her love moves her faith to a deeper level of listening and to its fruit, interior freedom. (*BP,* 19–20)

Luke 11:28 NKJV

Blessed are those who hear the word of God
and keep it!

· *February 4* ·

Word of Wisdom for Mary of Bethany

Trust in the LORD with all your heart....
Proverbs 3:5 NRSV

Jesus had a word of wisdom for Martha to help her in her difficulties. He also had a word of wisdom for Mary to help her to advance. When Jesus said, "Mary has chosen the *better* part," was he not inviting her to pursue the *best* part? Thus, he was encouraging her to still greater self-surrender and trust. (*BP*, 20)

Proverbs 3:5–6 NRSV

Trust in the LORD with all your heart,
and do not rely on your own insight.
In all your ways acknowledge him,
and he will make straight your paths.

· *February 5* ·

Surrender to the Unknown

My heart is open to the Spirit.

In the Gospel of John we find out that Lazarus was suffering from a serious illness. When he becomes deathly ill, the sisters send a message to Jesus saying, "Master, the one whom you love is sick" (John 11:3)....But Jesus does not come. He deliberately waits four days. Finally he acknowledged to the disciples, "Lazarus is dead....Now let us go to him!" Thus, he who cured thousands of others declined to make any effort to save the life of his special friend! How are we to understand Jesus' apparent indifference? What grief and despair did Lazarus feel in his last hours, knowing that Jesus could have come and did not come? This divine action challenges our *idea* of God, our *idea* of Jesus Christ, our *idea* of the spiritual life. Surrender to the unknown marks the great transitions of the spiritual journey. On the brink of each new breakthrough there is a crisis of trust and of love. (*BP*, 20–21)

John 11:40 NAB

Jesus said to her, "Did I not tell you that if you believe you would see the glory of God?"

· *February 6* ·

Word of Wisdom for Lazarus

Show me the way, Heart of my heart.

What was the mysterious illness from which Lazarus suffered and died? It was the death of his false self. Death is the only cure for the false self. That is why Jesus did not come. Only the death of the false self brings liberation from the drives for survival and security, affection and esteem, and power and control, and from overidentification with a particular group or role.... Lazarus, then, is a paradigm of Christian transformation. The spiritual meaning of Lazarus for us is that we cannot enter into the transforming union (or heaven) with our false selves. Lazarus in the tomb represents someone in the Night of Spirit who feels imprisoned [and] forgotten by God.... God returns at the appropriate time to call us forth from our darkness, confinement, loneliness, dereliction, and grief. Jesus' loud cry ordering Lazarus to come forth from the tomb was the word of wisdom Jesus saved for him. (*BP,* 22–23, 25)

John 11:43 NAB

[Jesus] cried out in a loud voice, "Lazarus, come out!"

· *February* 7 ·

Contemplative Service

Love turns work into rest.
Saint Teresa of Avila

Every time there is significant growth in our spiritual development all our relationships change — to God, to ourselves, to other people, and to all creation. We become a new person, as did Mary of Bethany at the feet of Jesus. From this arises a new kind of activity which might be called "contemplative service." Contemplative service is service that comes from the experience of the divine indwelling — from the Spirit living and at work within us. It is God in us serving God in others. (*BP*, 25–26)

Ephesians 6:7 NIV

Serve wholeheartedly,
as if you were serving the Lord....

· *February 8* ·

Contemplative Path in All Its Fullness

God, thank You for Your Presence.

Let us try to grasp the significance of Mary's gesture.
For her, Jesus' body was the alabaster jar filled with the
priceless perfume of the Holy Spirit. His body was to be
broken so that the fullness of the Holy Spirit dwelling
in him might be poured out over humanity. . . . Mary of
Bethany was inspired by the Holy Spirit to express her
boundless love in this dramatic and total way. In doing
so, she anticipated in her own person the passion, death,
and resurrection of Jesus. At the same time she manifested the unfolding of the contemplative path in all its
fullness. Contemplation is not only prayer but action
as well. And not only prayer and action, but the gift of
one's inmost being and all that one is. We are to allow
God to be God in us. (*BP*, 28–29)

John 12:3 NRSV

Mary took a pound of costly perfume made of pure nard,
anointed Jesus' feet, and wiped them with her hair. The
house was filled with the fragrance of the perfume.

· *February 9* ·

Scripture Acquaints Us with Jesus

Mary . . . sat . . . and listened. . . .
Luke 10:39 NRSV

What Mary of Bethany seems to be doing at the feet of
Jesus is practicing what came to be called Lectio Divina. This Latin phrase means "reading," or more exactly
"listening," to the book we believe to be divinely inspired. She is listening to Jesus' teaching. She is getting
acquainted, finding out what he thinks, what he likes
and does not like. We too can read Scripture to find out
who Jesus is, what he likes and what he does not like. To
get acquainted is to develop a personal relationship with
someone towards whom we feel an attraction. The reading of Scripture is the basis and support for all our ways
of relating with God. However developed our contemplative or meditative practices may become, they still
need to be nourished by Scripture. (*BP*, 31)

Luke 10:39 NRSV

Mary . . . sat at the Lord's feet
and listened to what he was saying.

· *February 10* ·

An Invitation

You . . . share in the divine nature. . . .
2 Peter 1:4 NAB

God's will for us is to manifest God's goodness and infinite tenderness in our lives right now. Christian tradition is not merely a handing on of various doctrines and rituals. It is the handing on of *the experience of the living Christ*, revealed in Scripture, preserved in the sacraments, renewed in every act of prayer, and present in a special way in the major events of our lives. If we are open and available to this presence, our lives will be transformed. The spiritual journey is a struggle to be ever more available to God and to let go of the obstacles to that transforming process. The Gospel is not merely an invitation to be a better person. It is an invitation to become divine. It invites us to share the interior life of the Trinity. (*BP*, 36–37)

2 Peter 1:4 NAB

He has bestowed on us the precious and very great promises, so that through them you may come to share in the divine nature. . . .

· *February 11* ·

Read Until You Feel the Call
of the Spirit

Ask...search...knock....
The door will be opened.
Matthew 7:7 NRSV

Lectio Divina leads to a personal relationship with God. The ancient monastic way of doing lectio does not mean reading a lot. It means reading the text until you feel the call of the Spirit either to reflect on a particular passage, sentence, or phrase, or to respond to the good things that you have read or heard. You may want to praise God, ask for something, or converse with God. Or you might feel like pouring out your heart to God. There is a movement from our concentrative practices to the receptive disposition that is essential for resting in God. (*BP*, 40)

Matthew 7:7–8 NRSV

Ask, and it will be given you; search, and you will find; knock, and the door will be opened for you. For everyone who asks receives, and everyone who searches finds, and for everyone who knocks, the door will be opened.

· *February 12* ·

Heart of Lectio Divina

Abide in His love.
John 15:10 NASB

Lectio Divina develops spontaneously if we do not get stuck on one of the stages of the process like over-intellectualizing or the multiplication of aspirations. The heart of the prayer is to recognize the presence and action of God and to consent to it. We do not have to go anywhere; God is already with us. Effort refers to the future and to what we do not yet have. Consent refers to the present moment and its content. Faith tells us that we already have God — the divine indwelling. The most intimate relationship with God is to be completely present to God in whatever we are doing. In this sense, prayer is a preparation for life. What we do in silence under ideal circumstances, we begin to do in daily life, remaining in the interior freedom we experienced during contemplative prayer even in the midst of intense activity. (*BP*, 41–42)

John 15:4 NIV

Remain in me, and I will remain in you.

· *February 13* ·

Effective Action

Let me sing God's song and dance God's dance.

Once the presence of God is a permanent part of daily life, there is a sense of spaciousness in the midst of all our activities. When difficulties arise because of events or other people, and our emotional reactions start to give us trouble, we can surround them with God's presence. This awareness relativizes the importance of the compulsion that we have to do something about every situation. Yes, we have to do something about certain situations, but if we do them from false self-motivation, we will not accomplish anything. When we act from the conviction of God's presence within us and with openness to the inspirations of the Holy Spirit, action becomes effective. (*BP*, 42)

Ephesians 3:20 NJB

Glory be to him whose power, working in us, can do infinitely more than we can ask or imagine....

· *February 14* ·

Look for the Fruits of the Spirit

By their fruits you will know them.
Matthew 7:16 NAB

Christian contemplation unfolds from the seeds of the graces planted at baptism. Among these are the Seven Gifts of the Spirit, all of which are oriented towards contemplative prayer and its development. Ordinarily, the Fruits of the Spirit appear first: charity, joy, peace, meekness, gentleness, long-suffering, goodness, patience, self-control (Gal. 5:23). If we are developing our friendship with Christ, these fruits are bound to appear. If they do not, we can question the seriousness or the depth of the relationship that we are having with Christ. (*BP,* 45–46)

Matthew 7:16–17 NAB

By their fruits you will know them....
Every good tree bears good fruit....

· *February 15* ·

Reduce the Obstacles

Learn to savor how good the LORD is....
Psalm 34:9 NAB

The Eucharist received in Holy Communion awakens us to the permanent presence of Christ within us at the deepest level. The Eucharist, like the Word of God in Scripture, has as its primary purpose to bring us to the awareness of God's abiding presence within us.... [Contemplative prayer] reduces the obstacles to the transforming energy of the Eucharist so that we can manifest in our attitudes and behavior the living Christ within us. As Jesus said, "He that loves me will in turn be loved by my Father; and I will love him and will manifest myself to him" (John 14:21).... If we do not have a discipline to reduce the obstacles in us to experiencing the presence of God, the full power of the sacraments are diluted and do not achieve their full potential to transform us. (*BP,* 55–56)

Hebrews 12:10 NIV

God disciplines us for our good,
that we may share in his holiness.

· *February 16* ·

Christ, the Divine Therapist

"The time has come.... The kingdom ... is near."
Mark 1:15 NIV

If we pray with the intention to open and surrender
to God, drawing the curtains on our ordinary thinking
processes for a specified time like half an hour, we are responding to Christ's call to repentance; that is, to change
the direction in which we are searching for happiness.
We are accepting Christ's invitation to a daily interview with him as the Divine Therapist. Through this
profoundly psycho-spiritual process, the Spirit works
back through our personal life history.... We access
each level until we come to the bottom where the real
source of most of our emotional problems actually is,
the fragility of early childhood. (*BP,* 62)

Mark 1:14–15 NIV

Jesus went into Galilee, proclaiming the good news of
God. "The time has come," he said. "The kingdom of
God is near. Repent and believe the good news!"

· *February 17* ·

God Knows Us and Loves Us

O Lord, You have searched me and known me.
Psalm 139:1 NASB

When we sit in Centering Prayer, introduce our sacred symbol, and enter a certain degree of rest, our defenses go down. The growth of interior silence along with our growing trust in God, enables us to face the dark side of our personality. We know that God knows us through and through, and still loves us. In fact, God could not be more delighted to provide this information. Grace enables us to evacuate negative emotions that are stuck in our nervous system, hindering the free flow of pure love that leads to divine transformation. (*BP*, 63)

Psalm 51:1–2 NLT

> Have mercy on me, O God,
> because of your unfailing love.
> Because of your great compassion,
> blot out the stain of my sins.
> Wash me clean from my guilt.
> Purify me from my sin.

· *February 18* ·

One with the Divine Presence

May they all be one....
John 17:21 NJB

Any practice moving towards contemplation is ecclesial in its effects. It bonds the people who are doing it with everybody else who is doing a similar practice, and indeed with everyone else in the human family. It creates community. As we sit in silence, we realize our oneness with others, not only with those with whom we pray, but with everyone on earth — past, present, and to come. What is deepest in them, their oneness with the divine presence, resonates with what is deepest in us. Hence, their joys, their trials, and their openness to God are part of us. (*BP*, 70)

John 17:21–22 NJB

May they all be one, just as, Father, you are in me and I am in you, so that they also may be in us.... I have given them the glory you gave me, that they may be one as we are one.

· *February 19* ·

Building Christian Community

Sir, give me this water. . . .
John 4:15 NRSV

In contemplative practice, as we pray together identifying ourselves with the Paschal Mystery, we believe that
Christ is in the center of the circle imparting to each
the special graces each one needs. The participants are
pooling their silence, so to speak, so that everyone gathered there can drink from this marvelous well of living
water that rises up from the center of the circle. Silence
in this context is liturgy of an exalted kind. We do not
say or do anything, but we engage in a special kind of
action that might be called alert receptivity. It is opening and consenting to God's presence and action within
us. (*BP*, 70–71)

John 4:14–15 NRSV

[Jesus said,] "Those who drink of the water that I will
give them will never be thirsty. The water that I will
give will become in them a spring of water gushing up
to eternal life." The woman said to him, "Sir, give me
this water, so that I may never be thirsty. . . ."

· *February 20* ·

The Divine Indwelling

The Spirit of God has made a home in you.
Romans 8:9 NJB

No amount of spiritual "yakking" can take the place of the intention to be with God at the deepest level of our being. This movement into our private room, into the innermost part of our being, is a movement of opening to the divine indwelling. The divine indwelling is the fundamental principle of relating to God in the Christian life, whether we are in prayer or action. (*BP,* 78)

John 14:23 NJB

Jesus replied:
Anyone who loves me will keep my word,
and my Father will love him,
and we shall come to him
and make a home in him.

· February 21 ·

Find God in the Present Moment

Today is the day of salvation.
2 Corinthians 6:2 NLT

During our private interview with the Divine Therapist, we are praying in secret. We settle into the present
moment which is the only place God actually is. God
is not in the past and not in the future. God is right
now, totally present, totally available. Our best response
is to be totally available to that presence. We surrender ourselves after the manner of Mary of Bethany.
She gave herself to Jesus, recognizing in him the fullness of the Spirit and the manifestation of the Father's
unconditional love. (*BP*, 82–83)

2 Corinthians 6:2 NLT

Indeed, God is ready to help you right now. Today is
the day of salvation.

· *February 22* ·

Pure Prayer versus False Self

[Pray] ... in ardent love for God. ...
Evagrius

Purity of heart was the primary objective of the practices of the desert fathers and mothers. They called contemplation "pure prayer," meaning prayer that is coming from a pure intention where the love of God is predominant. They did not seek for any reward such as consolation or enlightenment, or practice for the sake of motives that have their source in the ego, however devout. In point of fact the ego is not devout at all, though it likes to think it is devout and tries to hide behind a variety of religious facades. The spiritual journey is designed to put to rest these facades. But the false self is incredibly clever. Its desires are "worldly." It wants security, affection and esteem, and power and control, as substitutes for waiting upon God in loving attentiveness. (*BP*, 89)

1 Peter 2:2–3 NIV

Like newborn babies, crave pure spiritual milk, so that by it you may grow up in your salvation, now that you have tasted that the Lord is good.

· *February 23* ·
_____

Practice Centering Prayer Faithfully

Come and share your master's happiness!
Matthew 25:21 NIV

The attraction to the center of our being is the awakening to the fact of the divine indwelling. It is not a
particular thought, reflection, or feeling, but a sense of
being loved or embraced by God. But these experiences
are transient and are not the end of the journey. They
are ways of orienting us towards what is to come. The
Spirit may impart them to some people in great abun-
dance. Others, however, have to live most of the time
without them. The main thing everyone can do is the
practice. If you do the practice of Centering Prayer reg-
ularly, it will do you. There is no substitute for twice a
day practice. Talking about it, writing about it, does not
do it. Doing it does. (*BP*, 91)

Matthew 25:21 NIV

His master replied, "Well done, good and faithful servant! You have been faithful with a few things; I will
put you in charge of many things. Come and share your
master's happiness!"

· *February 24* ·

Scheduling Time for Prayer

There is a time for everything....
Ecclesiastes 3:1 NIV

Many people have found that contemplative prayer puts a certain order into their lives. As their minds became clearer and less cluttered, they are better able to choose their priorities. By giving time to contemplative prayer they actually have more time, because they stop doing things that before were useless or unnecessary. John of the Cross has this challenging saying, "If you find that you are working so much that you don't have enough time for your regular time of prayer, just double it!" (*BP*, 96)

Ecclesiastes 3:1, 7 NIV

There is a time for everything,
and a season for every activity under heaven:...
a time to be silent and a time to speak....

· February 25 ·

Guard of the Heart

Above all else, guard your heart....
Proverbs 4:23 NIV

Lectio Divina was discussed as a means of support-
ing and nourishing...contemplative prayer. Another
excellent practice is called Guard of the Heart. It is a
watchfulness that notices when we lose our sense of
peace. We lose peace whenever one of the emotional
programs for happiness is frustrated. Then grief, anger,
aversion, discouragement, and other afflictive emotions
go off. Once afflictive emotions go off, the imagination
provides prerecorded tapes that arise of themselves and
reinforce the intensity of the emotion. The two are like
the wheels of an old clock with interlocking teeth. If
one wheel turns, the other has to turn. Accordingly, if
you experience a strong emotion, in a second or two you
will find yourself with a commentary that is appropriate to it.... Commentaries...increase the intensity of
the original emotion.... If we learn to let go of afflictive emotions as promptly as they arise, we will enjoy a
more durable peace of mind. (*BP,* 97)

Proverbs 4:23 NIV

Above all else, guard your heart,
for it is the wellspring of life.

· *February 26* ·

Active Prayer Sentence

[Here's]...a formula of salvation...
Abba Isaac

Sometimes we may notice a pattern of getting upset in particular circumstances. We can then sleuth back and identify what the particular emotional program for happiness in the unconscious probably is. If you don't have time to go through that process, it may be simpler just to use another practice we call an Active Prayer Sentence. It is like the Jesus prayer, a prayer that you say over and over again until it says itself. John Cassian affirms that the monks of the desert used to sit in their cells weaving baskets saying constantly, "Oh God, come to my assistance. Oh Lord, make haste to help me." Perhaps the more mature monks would just say "Help." (*BP*, 98)

Psalm 70:1 NLT

Please, God, rescue me!
Come quickly, LORD, and help me.

· *February 27* ·

Another Way to Deepen Your Daily Practice

In quietness and . . . trust shall be . . . strength.
Isaiah 30:15 NRSV

A retreat once a year would deepen your daily practice, especially if the retreat is long enough, like five or
preferably eight full days. If that is not possible because
of your situation and responsibilities, take a retreat day
once a month, preferably along with others doing the
same kind of prayer practice. The support of similarly
minded people helps to persevere in prayer in difficult
times. (*BP*, 100)

Isaiah 30:15 NRSV

For thus said the Lord GOD, the Holy One of Israel: In
returning and rest you shall be saved; in quietness and
in trust shall be your strength.

· *February 28* ·

Reach out and Support Each Other

Go in peace to love and serve the world.
Dismissal from Mass

The love of God is so powerful that no one can just sit on it. It is bound to express itself. We have to think not just of praying together but how we can reach out and support each other in helping those in prison, the homeless, the hungry, the oppressed, everyone in need. Above all, direct attention to the most unbearable problem in the world today, which is the destitution of the poor. Jesus said: "The poor you will always have with you." But destitution is something else. That is our responsibility. It is not God's will.... The Spirit may be asking the Christian denominations to join forces with each other and with the other world religions in addressing human needs and social issues. The God in us is calling us to serve the God in others. (*BP,* 127–28)

Colossians 3:24 NJB

It is Christ the Lord that you are serving.

· *March 1* ·

Inner Conversion

The kingdom of God is at hand. Repent....
Mark 1:15 NAB

Into the human predicament — and the liturgical season of Lent — Jesus comes proclaiming, "Repent, for the reign of God is at hand." "Repent" means "change the direction in which you are looking for happiness." The call to repentance is the invitation to take stock of our emotional programs for happiness based on instinctual needs and to change them. This is the fundamental program of Lent. Year by year, as the spiritual journey evolves, the destructive influences of these unevaluated programs for happiness become more obvious and, in proportionate manner, the urgency to change them increases. Thus the process of conversion is initiated and carried on. The term of this process is the experience of inner resurrection celebrated in the Easter-Ascension Mystery. (*MC*, 37)

Mark 1:15 NAB

This is the time of fulfillment.
The kingdom of God is at hand.
Repent, and believe in the gospel.

· *March 2* ·

Temptations of Jesus

He himself suffered when he was tempted....
Hebrews 2:18 NIV

The Lenten liturgy begins with the temptations of Jesus in the desert, which deal with the three areas of instinctual need that every human being experiences in growing up. Jesus was tempted to satisfy his bodily hunger by seeking security in magic rather than in God; to jump off the pinnacle of the temple in order to make a name for himself as a wonder-worker; and to fall down and worship Satan in order to receive in exchange absolute power over the nations of the world. Security, esteem, power — these are three classic areas where temptation works on our false programs for happiness. (*MC*, 37)

Hebrews 2:18 NIV

Because he himself suffered when he was tempted, he is able to help those who are being tempted.

· March 3 ·

Responsibility for Our Emotional Life

The answer is in Jesus Christ....
Romans 7:25 NLT

The Gospel calls us forth to full responsibility for our emotional life. We tend to blame other people or situations for the turmoil we experience. In actual fact, upsetting emotions prove beyond any doubt that the problem is in us. If we do not assume responsibility for our emotional programs on the unconscious level and take measures to change them, we will be influenced by them to the end of our lives. As long as these programs are in place, we cannot hear other people and their cries for help; their problems must first be filtered through our own emotional needs, reactions and prepackaged values.... The heart of the Christian ascesis — and the work of Lent — is to face the unconscious values that underlie the emotional programs for happiness and *to change them.* Hence the need of a discipline of contemplative prayer and action. (*MC*, 39)

Romans 7:24–25 NLT

Oh, what a miserable person I am! Who will free me from this life that is dominated by sin? Thank God! The answer is in Jesus Christ our Lord.

· *March 4* ·

Biblical Desert: Interior Purification

Sit alone in silence....
Lamentations 3:28 NIV

Lent is the season in which the church as a whole enters into an extended retreat. Jesus went into the desert for forty days and forty nights. The practice of Lent is a participation in Jesus' solitude, silence and privation. The forty days of Lent bring into focus a long biblical tradition beginning with the Flood in the Book of Genesis, when rain fell upon the earth for forty days and forty nights. We read about Elijah walking forty days and forty nights to the mountain of God, Mt. Horeb. We read about the forty years that the Israelites wandered through the desert in order to reach the Promised Land. The biblical desert is primarily a place of purification, a place of passage. The biblical desert is not so much a geographical location — a place of sand, stones or sagebrush — as a process of interior purification leading to the complete liberation from the false-self system with its programs for happiness that cannot possibly work. (*MC*, 40)

Lamentations 3:25–26, 28 NIV

The LORD is good to those whose hope is in him, to the one who seeks him; it is good to wait quietly for the salvation of the LORD.... Sit alone in silence....

· *March 5* ·

The Human Condition

God...lead me along the path of...life.
Psalm 139:24 NLT

Jesus deliberately took upon himself the human condition — fragile, broken, alienated from God and other people. A whole program of self-centered concerns has been built up around our instinctual needs and have become energy centers — sources of motivation around which our emotions, thoughts and behavior patterns circulate like planets around the sun. Whether consciously or unconsciously, these programs for happiness influence our view of the world and our relationship with God, nature, other people and ourselves. This is the situation that Jesus went into the desert to heal. During Lent our work is to confront these programs for happiness and to detach ourselves from them. The scripture readings chosen for Lent and the example of Jesus encourage us in this struggle for inner freedom and conversion. (*MC*, 40–41)

Psalm 139:23–24 NLT

Search me, O God, and know my heart;
test me and know my thoughts.
Point out anything in me that offends you,
and lead me along the path of everlasting life.

· *March 6* ·

Confront the False Self

Let your ... love surround us, LORD....
Psalm 33:22 NLT

Each Lent [Jesus] ... invites us to join him in the desert and to share his trials. The Lenten observances are designed to facilitate the reduction of our emotional investment in the programs of early childhood. Liberation from the entire false-self system is the ultimate purpose of Lent. This process always has Easter as its goal. The primary observance of Lent is to confront the false self. Fasting, prayer and almsgiving are in the service of this project. As we dismantle our emotional programs for happiness, the obstacles to the risen life of Jesus fall away, and our hearts are prepared for the infusion of divine life at Easter. (*MC*, 42)

Hebrews 4:15–16 NLT

[Jesus] ... understands our weaknesses, for he faced all the same temptations we do, yet he did not sin. So let us come boldly to the throne of our gracious God. There we will receive his mercy, and we will find grace to help us when we need it.

· *March 7* ·

The Transfiguration

Loving Jesus, show me Your face.

[The text of the Transfiguration] is the continuation of
the invitation of Lent to undertake the inner purification that is required for divine union. On the mountain
Jesus was "transfigured," that is to say, the divine Source
of his human personality poured out through every pore
of his body in the form of light. His face became dazzling as the sun. Even his clothes shared in the radiance
of the inner glory that was flowing out through his body.
By choosing this text for the second Sunday of Lent,
the liturgy points to the fruit of struggling with the
temptations arising from our conscious or unconscious
emotional programming and of dying to the false-self
system. Repentance leads to contemplation. (*MC*, 43)

Matthew 17:2 NRSV

And he was transfigured before them,
and his face shone like the sun,
and his clothes became dazzling white.

· March 8 ·

Growing in Faith

Jesus . . . led them up a high mountain. . . .
Matthew 17:1 NRSV

The apostles . . . are paradigms of the developing consciousness of those who are growing in faith. . . . At first they are overjoyed by the sensible consolation that floods their bodies and minds in the presence of the vision of Christ's glory. Then the implications of this new world with its demands dawns upon them, and they are terrified. At the end of the vision, they experienced the reassurance of Jesus' presence and touch. This presence vastly surpassed the ephemeral sweetness of their initial taste of sensible consolation. Their exterior and interior senses were quieted by the awesomeness of the Mystery manifested by the voice out of the cloud. Once their senses had been calmed and integrated into the spiritual experience which their intuitive faculties had perceived, peace was established throughout their whole being, and they were prepared to respond to the guidance of the Spirit. (*MC*, 44)

Matthew 17:1 NRSV

Jesus took with him Peter and James and his brother John and led them up a high mountain, by themselves.

· *March 9* ·

Awakening to the Divine Presence

This is My beloved Son.... Hear Him.
Matthew 17:5 NKJV

The ideal disposition for the divine encounter is the gathering together of one's whole being in silent and alert attentiveness. The practice of interior silence produces gradually what the voice in the vision produced instantly: the capacity to listen. It withdraws the false self from its self-centeredness and allows the true self to emerge into our awareness. Revelation, in the fullest sense of the term, is our personal awakening to Christ. The external word of God and the liturgy dispose us for the experience of Christ's risen life within us. It is to this that the spiritual exercises of Lent are ordered. The awakening to the divine Presence emerges from what Meister Eckhardt called "the ground of being" — that level of being which in Christ is divine by nature and which in us is divine by participation. (*MC*, 45)

Matthew 17:5 NAB

A bright cloud cast a shadow over them, then from the cloud came a voice that said, "This is my beloved Son, with whom I am well pleased; listen to him."

· *March 10* ·

The Prodigal Son

Everything I have is yours.
Luke 15:31 NLT

The chief point of... [the Parable of the Prodigal Son]
is the invitation to each of us (whichever son you wish
to identify with) to recognize that the reign of God is
sheer gift. The divine inheritance does not belong to us
or anyone else. It is the result of the sheer goodness of
our Father. The father in this parable is characterized by
unconditional love toward both his sons, each of whom
abused the inheritance by wanting to take possession
of it in his own way. Each is equally guilty of rejecting
the goodness and love of this extraordinary father who
is not put off by either of them; neither by the wild
dissipation of the younger son, nor by the bitter self-
righteousness of the elder. The Elder Son is offered just
as much mercy as the younger, but because of his self-
righteousness, it is harder for him to receive it. His pride
will not allow him to accept the inheritance as sheer gift.
(*MC*, 49–50)

Luke 15:20 NLT

Filled with love and compassion,
he ran to his son, embraced him, and kissed him.

· *March 11* ·

The Spiritual Journey

Serve one another in love.
Galatians 5:13 NLT

[The Martha-Mary] parable encourages us to seek the integration of action and prayer. The time of contemplative prayer is the place of encounter between the creative vision of union with Christ and its incarnation in daily life. Without this daily confrontation, the contemplative vision can stagnate into a privatized game of perfectionism or succumb to the subtle poison of seeking one's own satisfaction in prayer. . . . Without the contemplative vision, daily renewed in contemplative prayer, action can become self-centered and forgetful of God. The contemplative dimension guarantees the union of Martha and Mary. This union is symbolized by Lazarus, who was the third member of the household. He is the symbol of the union of the active and contemplative lives. The mysterious illness that led to his death was self-knowledge, the awareness of his false-self system. As the risen life of Christ emerges from the ashes of his false-self system, he enters into the freedom and joy of divine life. (*MC*, 51–52)

Galatians 5:13 NLT

For you have been called to live in freedom — not freedom to satisfy your sinful nature, but freedom to serve one another in love.

· *March 12* ·

Love That Is Totally Self-Giving

Jesus, help me to spread your fragrance....
Cardinal Newman Prayer

[In the anointing at Bethany] Mary manifests her intuition into what Jesus is about to do. Moreover, she identifies with him to such an intimate degree that she manifests the same disposition of total self-giving that he is about to manifest on the cross. She had learned from Jesus how to throw herself away and become like God. That is why this story must be proclaimed wherever the Gospel is preached. "To perpetuate Mary's memory" is to fill the whole world with the perfume of God's love, the love that is totally self-giving. In the concrete, it is to anoint the poor and the afflicted, the favored members of Christ's Body, with this love. (*MC*, 55)

2 Corinthians 2:14–15 NASB

God...manifests through us the sweet aroma of... [Christ]....For we are a fragrance of Christ to God among [all]....

· *March 13* ·

Ultimate State to Which We Are Called

Christ calls me to be one with God.

Christ is the way to the Father. His human nature and personality is the door to his divinity. By identification with him as a human being, we find our true self — the divine life within us — and begin the process of integration into the life of the Father, Son and Holy Spirit. . . . The ultimate state to which we are called is beyond any fixed point of reference such as a self. . . . The death of Jesus on the cross was the death of his personal self, which in his case was a deified self. Christ's resurrection and ascension is his passage into the Ultimate Reality: the sacrifice and loss of his deified self to become one with the Godhead. . . . Union with Christ on the cross — our entrance into his experience — leads to the death of our separate-self sense. To embrace the cross of Christ is to be willing to leave behind the self as a fixed point of reference. It is to die to all separation, even to a self that has been transformed. It is to be one with God, not just to experience it. (*MC,* 56–57)

Luke 9:23 NLT

If any of you wants to be my follower, you must put aside your selfish ambition, shoulder your cross daily, and follow me.

· *March 14* ·

The Agony in the Garden

Remain here and keep watch with me.
Matthew 26:38 NAB

Jesus took upon himself the human condition more and more concretely as his life progressed. In the Garden of Gethsemani, he took upon himself the sin of the world with all its consequences. He experienced every level of loneliness, guilt and anguish that you or I or any human being has ever felt. The ghastly sum of accumulated human misery, sin and guilt descended upon him. He felt himself being asked by his Father to identify with this misery in all its immensity and horror.... After pleading in vain to the apostles to watch one hour with him, he withdrew a little way from them and fell on his face crying out, "Abba, if it be possible, let this chalice pass from me!" The clear realization that he was being asked by the Father to thrust himself as far from him as anyone has ever experienced, caused him unimaginable agony. By absorbing the separate-self sense into his inmost being, Jesus *became* sin. As Paul writes, "He who knew not sin was made sin for our salvation." (*MC*, 60)

Matthew 26:39 NAB

[Jesus] ... fell prostrate in prayer, saying, "My Father, if it is possible, let this cup pass from me; yet, not as I will, but as you will."

· March 15 ·

Jesus' Sacrifice

Christ . . . is in everything.
Colossians 3:11 NJB

As Jesus approached the end of his physical endurance on the cross, he cried out, "My God, my God, why have you forsaken me?" With these words, he revealed the fact that the act of taking upon himself the entire weight of human sinfulness had cost him the loss of his personal union with the Father. It is the final stage of Jesus' spiritual journey. This double-bind [an agonizing problem of facing two opposing goods], when it was resolved at the moment of his resurrection, catapulted him into a state of being beyond the personal union with the Father which had been his whole life until then. While his sacrifice opened up for the whole human family the possibility of sharing in his experience of personal union with the Father, it opened up for him a totally new level of being. His humanity was glorified to such a degree that he could enter the heart of all creation as its Source. Now he is present everywhere, in the inmost being of all creation, transcending time and space and bringing the transmission of divine life to its ultimate fulfillment. (*MC*, 61)

Colossians 3:11 NJB

Christ . . . is everything and he is in everything.

· March 16 ·

How Can I, Your Son, Become Sin?

God so loved the world. . . .
John 3:16 NAB

To become sin is to cease to be God's son — or at least
to cease to be conscious of being God's son. To cease
to be conscious of being God's son is to cease to experience God as Father. The cross of Jesus represents
the ultimate death-of-God experience. . . . The crucifixion is much more than the physical death of Jesus and
the emotional and mental anguish that accompanied it.
It is the death of his relationship with the Father. The
crucifixion was not the death of his false self because he
never had one. It was the death of his deified self and
the annihilation of the ineffable union which he enjoyed
with the Father in his human faculties. (*MC,* 62)

2 Corinthians 5:21 NAB

For our sake . . . [God] made . . . [Christ] to be sin who
did not know sin, so that we might become the righteousness of God in him.

· *March 17* ·

Paschal Mystery

Christ, our Passover Lamb, . . . [transform me.]
1 Corinthians 5:7 NLT

This passing of Jesus from human to divine subjectivity
is called in Christian tradition the Paschal Mystery. Our
participation in this Mystery is the passing over of the
transformed self into the loss of self as a fixed point of
reference; of *who* God is into *all that* God is. The dismantling of the false self and the inward journey to the
true self is the first phase of this transition or passing
over. The loss of the true self as a fixed point of reference is the second phase. The first phase results in the
consciousness of personal union with the Trinity. The
second phase consists in being emptied of this union and
identifying with the absolute nothingness from which
all things emerge, to which all things return, and which
manifests Itself as *That-Which-Is*. (MC, 62)

Philippians 2:5, 7–8 NRSV

Let the same mind be in you that was in Christ Jesus . . .
emptied . . . humbled . . . obedient. . . .

· *March 18* ·

God Rested from All His Work

He rested from all His work....
Genesis 2:3 NKJV

Jesus died on the day before the Sabbath. His body was taken down in a hurry and laid in the tomb. The Sabbath commemorates the seventh day of creation, the day God rested from all his works. In honor of creation and at God's express command, the Jewish people observed the Sabbath as a day of complete rest. But its most profound meaning is contained in this particular Sabbath in which, having laid down his life for the human family, Jesus, the Son of God, rested. Out of respect for the death of the Redeemer, there is no liturgical celebration on Holy Saturday. In honor of Jesus' body resting in the tomb, the church also rests. There is nothing more to be said, nothing more to be done. On this day everything rests. (*MC*, 63)

Isaiah 14:7 NRSV

The whole earth is at rest and quiet....

· *March 19* ·

Body of Jesus Anointed

Your anointing oils are fragrant....
Song of Solomon 1:3 NRSV

The text [John 19:38–42] describes Nicodemus and the holy women anointing Christ's body with a generous portion of myrrh, aloes and perfumed oils in accordance with the Jewish custom.... Perfumed oil... implies not only the bestowal of the Holy Spirit, symbolized by the anointing with oil, but also the *perception* of the presence and action of the Spirit, symbolized by the delicious odor of the perfume.... The outpouring of the Spirit as the fruit of Christ's sacrifice on the cross is magnificently expressed by Mary's lavish gesture.... Jesus' prophetic praise of Mary's action was thus thoroughly fulfilled: "What she has done is in anticipation of my burial." (*MC*, 65)

John 19:39–40 NRSV

Nicodemus ... came, bringing a mixture of myrrh and aloes, weighing about a hundred pounds. They took the body of Jesus and wrapped it with the spices in linen cloths, according to the burial custom of the Jews.

· *March 20* ·

He Has Risen

He has risen, he is not here.
Mark 16:6 NJB

His holy soul, bearing our sins, descended into the destructive waters of the Great Abyss in order that our
sinfulness might be utterly destroyed. . . . As Christ's soul
emerged from the waters made life-giving by the touch
of his sacred humanity and re-entered his body, the sacrifice he had offered released within the bosom of the
Father an incredible outpouring of divine light, life and
love. The fire of the Holy Spirit, bursting with the fullness of divine energy, rushed upon his sacred remains.
The perfumed oil of immense weight and value, sym-
bolizing the Spirit, suggests the immense power that
the Spirit exerted when the soul of Christ re-entered
his body. In this reunion, the Father poured into the
risen Jesus the whole of the divine essence — the utter
riches, glory, and prerogatives of the divine nature — in
a way that is utterly inconceivable to us. (*MC*, 67–68)

Revelation 2:18 NJB

The Son of God . . . has eyes like a burning flame
and feet like burnished bronze. . . .

· *March 21* ·

The Paschal Vigil

Light my way, Lord.

The reunion of the body and soul of Jesus took place in the secret of the night just before dawn, a moment that no one saw or witnessed. This is the event that is celebrated during the Paschal Vigil. The first rite of that sacred ceremony . . . is the blessing of the New Fire, the symbol of the Spirit descending upon the precious blood of Christ poured out upon the ground. A spark is taken from the New Fire to light the Paschal Candle, celebrating the moment that Christ rose from the dead in glory. The Paschal Candle is the symbol of the pillar of fire by which God led the Israelites out of the slavery of Egypt into the Promised Land. The same presence and action is now leading us from sin and disbelief to higher levels of faith and consciousness. (*MC*, 68)

Exodus 13:21 NRSV

The LORD went in front of them in a pillar of cloud by day, to lead them along the way, and in a pillar of fire by night, to give them light, so that they might travel by day and by night.

· *March 22* ·

Living Flame of Love

O living flame of love....
Saint John of the Cross

The Paschal Candle symbolizes the risen Christ leading his people to the promised land of divine transformation. As the single flame atop the Paschal Candle is shared and becomes the possession of each member of the assembly, the whole church is gradually illumined without the original flame being diminished. Divine charity, the ripe fruit of Christ's resurrection, never diminishes; it is increased by being shared. Because of the intrinsic power of the Easter mystery, the Paschal Vigil is not a mere commemoration of Christ's resurrection; it awakens the experience of Christ rising in our inmost being and spreading the fire of his love throughout all our faculties. (*MC*, 68)

1 John 4:11–12 NAB

Beloved, if God so loved us, we also must love one another. No one has ever seen God. Yet, if we love one another, God remains in us, and his love is brought to perfection in us.

· March 23 ·

Exultet, the Great Hymn of Easter

There is now no condemnation....
Romans 8:1 NASB

The great hymn of Easter is sung by the deacon....Notice in the hymn there is the statement that this sacred night "restores lost innocence." This phrase, of course, refers to the Garden of Eden and the story of Adam and Eve. It recalls their loss of intimacy with God. The heart of the Easter mystery is our personal discovery of intimacy with God which scripture calls "innocence." It is the innocence arising from easy and continual exchange of the most delightful kind with God....The spiritual journey is a way of remembering our Source, what Meister Eckhardt calls the "ground unconscious." The ground unconscious becoming conscious is our awakening to the Mystery of God's presence within us. This is the innocence to which scripture and the *Exultet* refer. (*MC*, 68–70)

Exultet, Paschal Vigil

The power of this night dispels all evil,
washes guilt away, and restores lost innocence....

· March 24 ·

The Resurrection of Jesus

We too . . . live in newness of life.
Romans 6:4 NAB

The resurrection of Jesus is the first day of the New Creation. The events following the resurrection and the various appearances of Jesus to his disciples and friends are used in the liturgy to help us understand the significance of this central Mystery of our faith. We have seen how Jesus died in the unresolved double-bind between identification with the human condition and the loss of personal union with the Father that is the inevitable result of this identification. The resurrection of Jesus is the resolution of that double-bind. It is the answer of the Father to the sacrifice of Jesus. It opened for us, as well as for him, a totally new life. It is the decisive moment in human history: as a result, divine union is now accessible to every human being. (*MC*, 71)

Romans 6:3–4 NAB

Or are you unaware that we who were baptized into Christ Jesus were baptized into his death? We were indeed buried with him through baptism into death, so that, just as Christ was raised from the dead by the glory of the Father, we too might live in newness of life.

· *March 25* ·

Intimacy and Union with God Restored

> I have seen the Lord....
> *John* 20:18 NRSV

The first resurrection scene is cast in a cosmic context. From the scriptural point of view, the garden in which the tomb of Jesus was situated reminds us of the garden of Eden. The two gardens are juxtaposed: in the first, the human family, in the persons of Adam and Eve, lost God's intimacy and friendship; in the second, Mary Magdalene (out of whom Jesus had cast seven devils) appears as the first recipient of the good news that intimacy and union with God are once again available. (*MC*, 71)

John 20:17–18 NRSV

Jesus said to her, "...Go to my brothers and say to them, 'I am ascending to my Father and your Father, to my God and your God.'" Mary Magdalene went and announced to the disciples, "I have seen the Lord"; and she told them that he had said these things to her.

· March 26 ·

The Interior State the Garden Represents

I love God and I know God loves me.

Adam and Eve were thrown out of the first garden as a result of the emergence of their self-consciousness apart from divine union. Mary [Magdalene] was so rooted in the experience of divine union that the Garden of Paradise was inside her and she could never leave it. The Garden of Eden stands for a state of consciousness, not a geographical location. She is sent out of the garden, but with the abiding interior state the garden represents: the certitude of being loved by God, of loving him in return, and of God giving himself in every event and at every moment, both within or without. (*MC*, 73–74)

Romans 8:38–39 NLT

And I am convinced that nothing can ever separate us from his love. Death can't, and life can't. The angels can't, and the demons can't. Our fears for today, our worries about tomorrow, and even the powers of hell can't keep God's love away. Whether we are high above the sky or in the deepest ocean, nothing in all creation will ever be able to separate us from the love of God that is revealed in Christ Jesus our Lord.

· March 27 ·

On the Road to Emmaus

Stay... the day is almost over.
Luke 24:29 NAB

The disciples could not recognize Jesus as long as their mindsets about who he was and what he was to do were in place. When Jesus demolished their blindness with his explanation of the scriptures, their vision of him began to assume a more realistic tone. The price of recognizing Jesus is always the same: our idea of him, of the church, of the spiritual journey, of God himself has to be shattered. To see with the eyes of faith we must be free of our culturally conditioned mindsets. When we let go of our private and limited vision, he who has been hidden from us by our pre-packaged values and pre-conceived ideas causes the scales to fall from our eyes. He was there all the time. Now at last we perceive his Presence. With the transformed vision of faith, we return to the humdrum routines and duties of daily life, but now... we recognize God giving himself to us in everyone and in everything. (*MC*, 77)

Luke 24:29–31 NAB

So he went in to stay with them. And it happened that, while he was with them at table, he took bread, said the blessing, broke it, and gave it to them. With that their eyes were opened and they recognized him....

· *March 28* ·

The Appearance in the Upper Room

Jesus . . . said to them, "Peace be with you."
John 20:19 NAB

In the midst of their conversation [in the upper room],
Jesus suddenly appeared, throwing the group into a state
of panic. They thought he was a ghost, even though
they had just been talking about his appearance to
Peter. Jesus' words to them are fraught with significance:
"Peace be to you!" Peace is the tranquility of order. It is
true security. True security is the direct consequence of
divine union. There is nothing wrong with desiring security. Everybody wants it and needs it. The problem is
that we look for it in the wrong places. Peace is the result
of the principal benefit of Christ's resurrection — the
experience of the divine Presence as permanent. Peace
is the treasure that Jesus triumphantly and joyfully be-
stows, or tries to bestow, on his crushed and demoralized
apostles. (*MC*, 78)

John 20:19 NAB

Jesus came and stood in their midst and said to them,
"Peace be with you."

· *March 29* ·

Christ Satisfies Thomas's Doubts

My Lord and my God!
John 20:28 NAB

Jesus said, "Thomas, let me have your finger. Put it here in my hands! And now let me have your hand. Place it here in my side!" Notice the detail with which Jesus meets his outrageous demands: point-by-point and word-for-word. "And do not be incredulous but believe!" That final remark pierced Thomas to the heart. He recognized the incredible goodness of Jesus in submitting himself to his demands. This loving acquiescence to every detail of his ridiculous demands placed Thomas in a state of complete vulnerability. Like Adam and Eve, he was being called out of the woods, out of the underbrush where his false self had been hiding from the truth, into the stark reality of Jesus' love. What could he say? His response was the total gift of himself: "My Master and my God!" (*MC*, 82)

John 20:28–29 NAB

Thomas answered and said to him, "My Lord and my God!" Jesus said to him, "Have you come to believe because you have seen me? Blessed are those who have not seen and have believed."

· *March 30* ·

Resurrection Appearance at Sea of Galilee

Spirit of God, I trust in You.

A meal together is a symbol of belonging. Before it had always meant conversation, laughter and singing. This was a new level of belonging. Their former relationship with Jesus was coming to an end and a new relationship was being communicated to them at a far deeper level. This sharing was not by word of mouth, nor by ideas or feelings, but by the Spirit dwelling in their inmost being, a far better form of communication than the one they had before. . . . The fifty days during which Jesus revealed himself to his disciples brought them out of their discouragement and into close relationship with the divine Spirit whom he had promised to send them. The disciples were brought from a merely human relationship with Jesus to the interior exchange that is proper to those who are advancing in faith and in sensitivity to the inspirations of the Spirit. (*MC*, 85–86)

John 21:12 NAB

Jesus said to them, "Come, have breakfast." And none of the disciples dared to ask him, "Who are you?" because they realized it was the Lord.

· March 31 ·

The Ascension

[Christ] . . . fills everything in every way.
Ephesians 1:23 NIV

The Ascension is Christ's return to the heart of all
creation where he dwells now in his glorified humanity. The mystery of his Presence is hidden throughout
creation and in every part of it. At some moment of
history, which prophecy calls the Last Day, our eyes
will be opened and we will see reality as it is, which we
know now only by faith. That faith reveals that Christ,
dwelling at the center of all creation and of each individual member of it, is transforming it and bringing it
back, in union with himself, into the bosom of the Father. Thus, the maximum glory of the Trinity is achieved
through the maximum sharing of the divine life with
every creature according to its capacity. (*MC*, 87)

Ephesians 1:23 NAB

The fullness of [Christ] . . . fills all things in every way.

· *April 1* ·

An Invitation to Go Deeper into the Heart of Christ

God has ... given us his Spirit. ...
1 Corinthians 2:12 NLT

There is an analogy between growing up spiritually and the growing up that takes place in the normal course of human life. In approaching adolescence and adulthood, everyone seems to have to pass through a crisis. ... God has great sympathy for those who are going through this crisis in their spiritual life. They do not know what is happening to them and tend to concentrate on the disintegration of what they love, rather than on the real spiritual growth of which they are becoming capable. ... If we look on the bright side and are firmly convinced that it is normal to have to forge new relationships, our crisis of faith will appear as a great invitation to go deeper into the heart of Christ. The very transition makes it impossible for the former people we counted on to help us. Part of growing up is to become independent — not of everybody, but of those on whom we are too dependent — so that we may depend completely on the Holy Spirit. That is what spiritual maturity is. (*CF,* 9, 13)

1 Corinthians 2:12, 14 NLT

God has actually given us his Spirit (not the world's spirit) so we can know the wonderful things God has freely given us. ... Only those who have the Spirit can understand what the Spirit means.

· *April 2* ·

Call to a New Relationship

The seed is the word of God.
Luke 8:11 NIV

At some point in our spiritual growth Jesus asks us to adjust ourselves to a new relationship with himself. Since this happens without much warning, almost no one has any awareness of what is taking place when it actually happens. It comes on gradually, slowly but surely. However, we can so successfully distract ourselves from our interior life that we actually never make the adjustment and never forge the new relationship Jesus asks of us. . . . Some people who have received a distinct gift for prayer lose it, because at the time of this transition they surrender to excessive activity, get fed up, or stumble over some obstacle to forging the new relationship. (*CF,* 11)

Luke 8:15 NIV

The seed on good soil stands for those with a noble and good heart, who hear the word, retain it, and by persevering produce a crop.

· April 3 ·

Jesus Responds to Different Degrees of Faith

We need more faith; tell us how to get it.
Luke 17:5 NLT

There are two great crises [faith and love] in the process of spiritual maturity.... For the present let us consider the ... crisis [of faith]. In John's gospel we have ... a royal official ... pleading, "Come down and heal my son!" Jesus showed great reluctance to go, saying, "Unless you see striking signs of power, you do not believe." But the man cried out in desperation, "Sir, come down now. My son is on the point of death!" Jesus replied, "You go. Your son is healed." ... At the same hour ... the very moment Jesus uttered the words, the fever left the boy. Another scene.... Along came a centurion and said to Jesus, "My slave is sick and is suffering frightfully." Jesus said, "I will come down right away and heal him." The centurion objected, "Oh no! Just say the word and my servant will be healed. I am unworthy that you should come under my roof." In these two instances we see Jesus adjusting himself to men possessing different degrees of faith. The first man believed in the power of Jesus' presence. His weak faith required the physical presence of Jesus. (*CF,* 14–15)

Matthew 8:8 NAB

Only say the word and my servant will be healed.

· April 4 ·

Opportunities to Grow in Faith

Give God a chance to increase our faith.

[The royal official]...is a symbol of those who need to feel the sensible presence of The Lord, at least from time to time to sustain their faith. And what does Jesus do? He refuses to go down. Why? Because...the absence of the felt presence of the Lord is his normal means of increasing our faith and of getting us to the point of believing in the power of his word alone, without "signs and wonders," that is to say, without the feeling of his presence or external props. It is a crisis of faith that he puts the royal official through, and with great success. From that time on, he believed.... [Jesus] wants very much to give us his gifts, but our weakness and our individual psychology requires that he proceed with caution, with a certain diplomacy. He can only give us what we are capable of receiving at the present moment. The events that he allows or causes to happen, if we respond with faith, give him the chance to increase our faith.... Each of us is more or less a problem to Jesus. He responds to us according to the degree of faith which we have right now. (*CF,* 15–16)

John 4:48 NLT

Must I do miraculous signs and wonders before you people will believe me?

· *April 5* ·

Crisis of Faith Is a Call to New Growth

[Jesus] said . . . "Launch out into the deep. . . ."
Luke 5:4 NKJV

He [Jesus] transforms a man's weak faith into a strong living faith. But only at the price of a crisis, at the price of death to his own desires and judgment. The physical presence of the Master which he [the royal official] wanted, and which he thought he needed, had first to be taken away. In our own spiritual growing up process we cannot escape the crisis of faith. This incident clearly teaches us that it is not merely a rebuke when Jesus seems to push us against the wall and to remove the props which we feel are so necessary for us. It is rather a call to new growth, to the transformation of our weakness. It is a call to a new union with him, a call to "launch out into the deep." (*CF,* 23)

Luke 5:4 NKJV

He [Jesus] said to Simon, "Launch out into the deep and let down your nets for a catch."

· *April 6* ·

Meet the Challenge

Your word is enough for me, Lord.

The great pity is that we so often fail to meet this challenge [a new union with Christ]. We bog down in our demands for Christ's felt presence or for other props to our faith. If we would allow them to go and believe in his word alone, in his divinity, we would then experience that transformation of our faith, the fruit of which is a new outpouring of the Holy Spirit, symbolized in John's gospel by the wine. Remember that the Holy Spirit is a spirit who cannot be attained by means of feelings or reasoning. By allowing the former kind of relationship to be taken away — or to be torn away — we make it possible for The Spirit to transform our faith into an abiding awareness of God. (*CF,* 23–24)

Psalm 88:14 NIV

Why, O LORD, do you reject me
and hide your face from me?

· *April 7* ·

Faith in the Power of His Word Alone

As you have believed, let it be done....
Matthew 8:13 NAB

By refusing the request of the royal official to go to heal his son, Jesus gave him the opportunity to rise to a higher degree of faith. The centurion was a man in almost exactly the same outward situation as the royal official. He also had someone, his slave, whom he wanted cured. Instead of refusing to go down, Jesus showed himself most willing and eager to oblige. He did this in order to give the centurion the opportunity to manifest the magnificent faith he had in the power of his word alone. It also gave Jesus the opportunity to bring that extraordinary faith to the attention of his disciples. (*CF,* 25)

Matthew 8:8 NAB

Lord, I am not worthy to have you enter under my roof; only say the word and my servant will be healed.

· April 8 ·

Trust in God's Mercy

Jesus, I trust in You.
Saint Maria Faustina Kowalska
(Diary, 327)

The Canaanite woman had the kind of faith which penetrates the clouds. She would not take any kind of refusal
as a real refusal, as a real "no." She kept on praying with
faith. The more she was tried, the more she placed her
trust in Jesus, until she finally achieved her goal and got
all she wanted. This is the disposition God waits for
in the crisis of faith: trust in his mercy no matter what
kind of treatment he gives you. Only great faith can
penetrate those apparent rebuffs, comprehend the love
which inspires them, and totally surrender to it. (*CF,* 29)

Matthew 15:24–27 NLT

Then he said to the woman, "I was sent only to help the
people of Israel — God's lost sheep — not the Gentiles."
But she came and worshiped him and pleaded again,
"Lord, help me!" "It isn't right to take food from the
children and throw it to the dogs," he said. "Yes, Lord,"
she replied, "but even dogs are permitted to eat crumbs
that fall beneath their master's table."

· April 9 ·

Silence Is a Real Answer

But He did not answer her a word....
Matthew 15:23 NASB

Review...the dialogue between Jesus and the Canaanite woman to bring out another aspect of the crisis of faith. The question to be answered is: what constitutes successful passage through the crisis of faith? This determined woman, I think you will agree, successfully passed through her crisis in a few moments. It will doubtless take us many months or years to negotiate ours. She came out of the district of Canaan crying, "Have pity on me, Son of David, because my daughter is sorely tormented by a demon!" Now the gospel says, "In answer to her, Jesus replied not a word." Let us observe these words rather closely. You will notice the gospel does not say he gave no response. Nor does it say he answered "yes" or "no" but simply: "In answer to her request, he did not say a word." In other words, as far as Jesus was concerned, silence, lack of response, is a real answer. (*CF,* 30)

Matthew 15:22–23 NAB

"Have pity on me, Lord, Son of David!
My daughter is tormented by a demon."
But he did not say a word in answer to her.

· *April 10* ·

Faith Grows into Confidence

O woman, great is your faith!
Matthew 15:28 NAB

When faith grows into confidence, the crisis of faith has done its work and the crisis itself is resolved. Deep interior peace reigns. The Lord does hear. The silence of Jesus is the ordinary means he uses to awaken in us that perfect confidence which leads to humility and love — and to gaining all that we ask.... What we really want and what the Holy Spirit is inspiring us to long for in the crisis of faith is a confrontation with the Word of God in our inmost being. It is contact with the divinity of Christ. It is to be brought inwardly face to face with the living God, who, faith assures us, dwells within us, and who, hope reassures us, will reward those who seek him with his presence. (*CF*, 32–33)

Matthew 15:28 NAB

Then Jesus said to her in reply, "O woman, great is your faith! Let it be done for you as you wish." And her daughter was healed from that hour.

· *April 11* ·

Develop Humility

Be patient as you wait for the Lord....
James 5:7 NLT

The habit of waiting for God gradually establishes us in a right attitude towards him. We cannot push God around. But that is what we try to do when we say, "Give me this; give me that." Or even, "Please, give me this." Some even make bold to say: "If you don't give me this, I won't say any more prayers." Or, "How can you do this to me?" But God's answer to all this is: "Well, who are you?" There is nothing so humbling as waiting — that is why time was created, so that we might learn to wait. Waiting makes you feel inferior to the person who is keeping you waiting. And this begins to dawn on you the longer you have to wait. That is why some people cannot stand it any more and get up and walk out. (*CF,* 38)

James 4:10 NKJV

Humble yourselves in the sight of the Lord, and He will lift you up.

· April 12 ·

Jesus Raises Lazarus from the Dead

Believe ... [and] see the glory of God....
John 11:40 NAB

Now let us turn to the dramatic event of the raising of Lazarus from the dead. This incident puts before us an interesting comparison between the faith of Martha and Mary.... When Jesus arrived at Bethany, he found that Lazarus had already been four days in the tomb.... Now notice the reaction of the two sisters. As soon as Martha heard that Jesus had arrived, she went out to meet him, but Mary remained at home.... Mary waited until he sent for her. Why should she go out to seek him whom she possessed within? ... Jesus is now asking Martha and Mary to believe that he can raise their brother from the dead. This is a bit too much for Martha. She has not quite reached this degree of faith. With her usual practical bent, she warns, "Master, his body stinks by this time. He has been dead four days." But Mary says nothing. Her faith holds out. Remember that Lazarus is a symbol of someone who has been Christ's friend and for whom everybody has given up hope — except Mary. It is her faith that Jesus is actually counting on in order to work this miracle. (*CF,* 39, 42–44)

John 11:40 NAB

Did I not tell you that if you believe you will see the glory of God?

· April 13 ·

Paradox of the Crisis of Faith

God...found by...not looking...not asking....
Romans 10:20 NLT

The purpose of the crisis of faith is to bring us to a radical willingness to live by faith alone and to give up the support of sensible consolations. Here is the paradox illustrated by comparing the royal official and the centurion, and then Martha and Mary: seek Jesus' sensible presence — a consoling presence you can feel and understand — and you will not find him. Give up seeking the consolation of his sensible presence, and you will find him. This idea is expressed by the text of Isaiah quoted in the Epistle to the Romans: "I was found by these who did not seek me. I revealed myself to those who made no inquiry about me." (*CF,* 45–46)

Romans 10:20 NLT

Isaiah spoke boldly for God:
"I was found by people
who were not looking for me.
I showed myself to those
who were not asking for me."

· April 14 ·

Willingness to Live by Faith Alone

Lord, I am grateful for growing faith.

The degree of spiritual maturity that corresponds to the passage from childhood to adolescence is the realization that Jesus is truly God and the full acceptance of that fact by seeking him by faith, without leaning on natural props and sensible consolations of one kind or another. Martha went to see him, that is to say, she went in search of his sensible presence; but Mary stayed home. Why? Because she possessed him already by faith. When she was sent for, then she was all ready to go. Her admirable discretion is worth observing, especially in the light of what follows. She went to meet Jesus at his call. She humbled herself before doing anything else. When she showed him her tears, Jesus completely melted and gave her more than she dared to ask for. (*CF,* 46)

John 11:41–44 NLT

Then Jesus looked up to heaven and said, "Father, thank you for hearing me. You always hear me, but I said it out loud for the sake of all these people standing here, so they will believe you sent me." Then Jesus shouted, "Lazarus, come out!" And Lazarus came out, bound in graveclothes. . . .

· *April 15* ·

Goal of Crisis of Faith: Total Surrender

She ... pleaded again, "Lord, help me!"
Matthew 15:25 NLT

Our own efforts can take us only so far [on the spiritual journey], then gradually their inadequacy shows up. We must be reduced step by step to the situation in which the Canaanite woman found herself when, despairing of all her own resources and with a desperation tempered only by hope in Jesus, she cried out from the bottom of her heart: "Help me!" Two little words which can express grades of meaning which are almost infinite, from the lip service of somebody who has read that one should depend on God, to somebody who has experienced the complete destruction and loss of all his own human resources and who turns to God utterly. This total surrender is the purpose and goal of the crisis of faith. (*CF,* 49–50)

John 12:24–25 NAB

Amen, amen, I say to you, unless a grain of wheat falls to the ground and dies, it remains just a grain of wheat; but if it dies, it produces much fruit. Whoever loves his life loses it, and whoever hates his life in this world will preserve it for eternal life.

· *April 16* ·

Growing Up in Grace

Be imitators...of Christ.
1 Corinthians 11:1 NASB

The idea of suffering becoming pure joy or stopping altogether is nonsense. To be a Christian, the gospel nowhere says that you must relish and savor all the anguish and suffering that can come upon you. Growing up in grace does not mean becoming inhuman or insensible. Jesus suffered as a human being. But there is this difference between him and us: he was prepared, out of love of his Father, to suffer anything that the Father wanted him to suffer. This is what the Canaanite woman did in the face of her outward humiliation and sufferings. She hung on, she trusted, she hoped against hope. These are the dispositions which are truly Christian and which indicate a high degree of spiritual maturity. When the theological virtues of faith, hope, and charity are the principal means by which we go to God, and we are willing to let all other means be taken away — or torn away — when God asks for them, then we are truly imitating Christ.... (*CF*, 52)

John 12:26 NLT

All those who want to be my disciples must come and follow me....And if they follow me, the Father will honor them.

· April 17 ·

Great Faith Moves to Great Love

Your faith has saved you. Go in peace.
Luke 7:50 NKJV

It was the forgiveness of her . . . sins that transformed . . .
[the penitent woman described in Luke 7:36–50] into
an ocean of love. . . . In this poor penitent woman, we
have an example of someone who does know her own
misery and wretchedness, and how sunk in sin she is,
who makes no secret of the fact to herself and to God
(and to everybody else for that matter), and who appeals
to the love of Christ to save her. . . . She just collapses
at his feet and relies a hundred percent on his mercy.
Imagine what she must have felt when Jesus turned to
her and said, "Your sins are forgiven." That is all she
wanted to hear. . . . He does not ask for anything except
the sincere acknowledgement of need, and hope in his
mercy. . . . Jesus then said to her, "Your faith has saved
you." Faith in what? *Faith in his love.* That is what saved
her. (*CF,* 57, 59)

Luke 7:48, 50 NKJV

Then He said to her, "Your sins are forgiven. . . .
Your faith has saved you. Go in peace."

· *April 18* ·

Praise Is the Fruit of Love

I will bless the LORD at all times....
Psalm 34:1 NRSV

Praise is the fruit of love. The heart of the Christian Community is on fire to praise God. It feels an urgent necessity to thank him, not just once in a while, but all the time, because of the graces he pours out on the world at every moment. The three women [Mary of Bethany, Mary Magdalen, and the penitent woman], commemorated in the feast of St. Mary Magdalen, and [psalmist] David, are all under the influence of the same grace. They are entering deeper into the heart of the Christian Community, the mystical body of Christ, and they have to praise God. It is a need of love and of gratitude. (*CF,* 62)

Psalm 34:1, 3 NRSV

I will bless the LORD at all times;
his praise shall continually be in my mouth....
O magnify the LORD with me,
and let us exalt his name together.

· April 19 ·

Spiritual Attentiveness

O taste and see that the LORD is good....
Psalm 34:8 NRSV

[Psalm 34:8]...suggests the mystery of love, the fact that we know God and attain to a deep knowledge of him through love rather than by intellectual reflection. ...According to the psalmist, we must first taste, enjoy, and then understand.... The spiritual senses are an analogy of the material ones: sight, hearing, touch and taste. In bodily things, taste and touch are the most intimate because an object is present directly when you taste or touch it. It is less directly present when you see it, hear it, or smell it. Touch is experienced when an object is present inwardly. God is substantially present in the inmost depths of our soul, and if he makes his presence felt there, the most appropriate analogy of it is taste — the most intimate, the most direct experiences of the senses. It is an analogy; not a sensible reality, but a spiritual experience. (*CF,* 63–64)

Psalm 34:8 NRSV

O taste and see that the LORD is good;
happy are those who take refuge in him.

· April 20 ·

Spiritual Sense of Smell

Myrrh is my beloved to me....
Song of Solomon 1:13 NKJV

The spiritual sense of smell is manifested by an inner attraction for prayer, solitude and silence — to be still and wait upon God with loving attention. This attraction draws us irresistibly to our encounter with Christ even when he does not show up for a long time. The words of the canticle, "Draw me, we will run after you in the odor of your delicious perfume," does not mean that we are going to experience the smell of delicious perfume. Rather, we experience the inner attraction of God *as if* his presence was a delicious odor arising from within and attracting us to him. We cannot control this perfume; we can only receive it or place ourselves in its path. It communicates itself on its own terms, when and as God wills. (*CF,* 67–68)

Song of Songs 1:3–4 NJB

Delicate is the fragrance of your perfume,
your name is an oil poured out....
Draw me in your footsteps, let us run.

· April 21 ·

Spiritual Sense of Touch

Kiss me with the kisses of his mouth. . . .
Song of Songs 1:2 THS

The spiritual sense of touch is more intimate than the sense of smell and the attraction to the delightful perfume of God's presence. The divine touch, like the divine perfume, is not a bodily sensation. Rather it is *as if* our spirit were touched by God or embraced. The divine touch might feel as if God were descending from above and enveloping us in an embrace, or embracing us from within, and placing a great big kiss in the middle of our spirit. Our own self-identity lets go, and for a moment God is all in all. The delight may overflow from this deep spiritual source into the external senses, and then the body also rejoices. The Spirit of God, can transform the entire organism into an immense celebration of love, peace, and joy. . . . (*CF,* 68–69)

Song of Songs 1:2 THS

Let him kiss me with the kisses of his mouth. . . .

· *April 22* ·

Full Development of the Spiritual Senses

Your . . . spirit is in everything!
Wisdom 12:1 NJB

It is one thing to be so close as to touch someone, another to penetrate the spirit of the other. Only God who dwells within can be experienced at such an intimate and profound level. When we taste something, we usually consume it and transform it into ourselves; it becomes a part of us. In divine union the presence of God arises not only as an irresistible attraction or embrace, but as a unifying presence in our inmost being. It is there that the grace of Pentecost takes place: Christ living our life, or more exactly, living us. When our whole being is rooted in God, we see him in everything and everything in him. This is not the fruit of one experience, at least not as a rule, but the full development of the spiritual senses. (*CF,* 69)

Wisdom 11:26, 12:1 NJB

All is yours, LORD, lover of life!
For your imperishable spirit is in everything!

· *April 23* ·

The Eucharist

Taste and see the goodness of the Lord.
Traditional Communion Hymn

Once we have accessed the experience of spiritual taste,
we can move back and forth among the spiritual senses
like the angels on Jacob's ladder, symbols of relating
to God at each level of our being.... [Jesus] communicated the interior perfume of his presence to Mary of
Bethany and the interior touch of divine union to John
[when John lay his head on the breast of Jesus at the Last
Supper]; however, God gave to all the apostles the grace
of divine union at the Last Supper by offering them the
bread and wine transformed into his physical and spiritual presence. Thus in receiving the Eucharist, we too
are offered the grace that corresponds to the spiritual
sense of taste, the highest form of spiritual awakening.
(*CF,* 69)

John 6:55–56 NJB

For my flesh is real food and my blood is real drink.
Whoever eats my flesh and drinks my blood lives in me
and I live in that person.

· *April 24* ·

Faith Leads to Pure Love of God

I desire nothing but to love You.
Saint Teresa of Avila

Beyond any experience, however spiritual and profound, remains the mystery of pure faith and pure love. This is our capacity to enter into divine union without self-reflection. God, the divine energy, is so powerful and so intimate that no human faculty can perceive it in its purity. But faith receives the grace of divine union by consent. The growing conviction, born of spiritual experience and the purification of contemplative prayer, gradually awakens us to the reality of faith as the narrow way that leads to the pure love of God. (*CF,* 70)

1 John 4:16–17 NLT

We know how much God loves us, and we have put our trust in him. God is love, and all who live in love live in God, and God lives in them. And as we live in God, our love grows more perfect.

· *April 25* ·

Purification of Love

Lovingly accept all . . . God sends us. . . .
Jean-Pierre de Caussade

Let us suppose . . . that we, by the grace of God, have had our faith purified and have experienced our hope and trust ripening into love. We know we love God and are seeking not so much his favors, but himself. Would you think that such a strong love still needed purification? Let us look at Mary, the mother of Jesus. One might think that she, at least, was perfect in love and grace from the beginning. But God's idea of love is different from ours. . . . Jesus says, "Why did you look for me? Didn't you know . . . that I had to be about my father's business?" . . . Even [Mary] . . . needed to be reminded by Jesus of the primacy of the Father's will. . . . When this gospel is proclaimed in the liturgy of the Christmas season, the prayer of the day asks that we be shown, "the good, the acceptable, and the perfect will of God." This prayer suggests that there are three degrees of submission to the will of God. The good will of God is his will above every other affection. And the perfect will of God is his will above every other love including ourselves. (*CF,* 72–75)

Psalm 40:8 NIV

I desire to do your will, O my God. . . .

· *April 26* ·

She Put in More Than All the Others

Lord, here's the gift of my heart.

From God's point of view, it is not accomplishments but efforts that count. If we accept our poverty and limitations, but still go on trying, we will rate higher than everybody else in God's book, just as the poor widow did.... If we make the effort and receive that one precious point for trying, God can take his pencil and start adding zeros after it. But if that crucial point is missing, no amount of zeros can help. Our score will be just plain "zero." What did Jesus mean when he said of the poor widow and her offering, "She put in more than all the others?" She actually put in only two small coins. But he knew that he was adding zeros so that she would turn up with the loving cup. She really got the first prize, but without knowing it. It never entered her mind that she was doing something great. (*CF*, 82)

Proverbs 23:26 NRSV

My child, give me your heart....

· *April 27* ·

The Mystery of Suffering

Blessed be the name of the LORD.
Job 1:21 KJV

There is a great mystery in the suffering of the innocent. Perhaps it is better just to accept it as a mystery rather than to try to explain it. Apparently Job did not take Satan into consideration in his complaints. Step by step, materially then spiritually, as you see from the text, especially as we read on, he is left with only one thread of consolation: the fact that God is God, the Creator who can do whatever he likes; and nobody can say to him, "You can't do that to me." As he is reduced gradually to the acceptance of that fact, and to silence, the purity of his love grows apace. In the end, God made Job twice as rich (...a symbol of his interior grace) as he was before his trials began. (*CF*, 88)

Job 1:21 KJV

Naked came I out of my mother's womb, and naked shall I return thither: the LORD gave, and the LORD hath taken away; blessed be the name of the LORD.

· April 28 ·

God Asks Two Sacrifices

Give thanks to the LORD, for he is good. . . .
Psalm 106:1 NIV

In the crisis of faith, God asks of us two sacrifices. One is the sacrifice of the desert, and the other is the sacrifice of praise. . . . The sacrifice of the desert is the sacrifice of bearing with temptation. When we experience the rebellion of our lower nature, we offer ourselves to God in the state of weakness, misery, and apparent defeat. . . . But there is also the sacrifice of praise. . . . From time to time in this desert we come to an oasis, and for a few moments God allows us to experience his love and to be conscious of his divine help. When we are up against it and have no strength of ourselves, and cast all our hope on him; or when we expect to fail but for some extraordinary reason, which can only be the grace of God, do not; then there wells up a flood of gratitude, very gentle at times, at other times like a tidal wave. Call it consolation if you wish. At least it is the consolation of not having failed, of not having surrendered to temptation and sin. (*CF,* 90)

Hebrews 13:15 NIV

Let us continually offer to God a sacrifice of praise — the fruit of lips that confess his name.

· *April 29* ·

Rest Comes to Those Who Love Much

My soul finds rest in God alone....
Psalm 62:1 NIV

The habit of referring everything to God and of flying
to him for refuge, together with the experience of being
delivered, has brought us a profound stability of soul. It
is the Sabbath rest, of which Sunday is the symbol, and
of which heaven is the perfect fulfillment.... The fullness of love brings the maximum of rest at the same time
that it makes possible the maximum of action. Mary, the
mother of Jesus, is the exemplar of this grace. That is
why, on the feast of the Assumption in the Cistercian
liturgy, the gospel of Mary and Martha is read. As the
perfect contemplative, she unites in herself the capacity
to work for God and to rest in God, which belongs to
those who have passed through the crisis of faith and of
love, and who have entered interiorly into the Sabbath
of the Lord. (*CF,* 94)

Hebrews 4:6 NLT

God's rest is there for people to enter.

· *April 30* ·

Lazarus: Symbol of Christian Awakening

Wake up...Christ will shine on you....
Ephesians 5:14 NJB

The story of Lazarus is a preview of Jesus' approaching death and resurrection. Lazarus stands for fallen man about to be raised from the death of sin to life in God through Christ's passion, death, and resurrection. The illness which Jesus allows Lazarus to undergo is the symbol of man's false self with all its weakness, ignorance, and pride, together with all the damage lying in the unconscious from earliest childhood to the present moment....Lazarus represents...those who seek to penetrate the mystery of Christ to its depth. The disposition is manifested by a willingness to die to the false self and to wait in patience for the inner resurrection, which can only come from Christ. (*CF,* 95)

Ephesians 5:14 NJB

Wake up, sleeper,
rise from the dead,
and Christ will shine on you.

· *May 1* ·

Letting Go of the False Self

Wash away my hidden faults.
Psalm 19:12 NJB

One of the biggest impediments to spiritual growth is that we do not perceive our own hidden motivations. Our unconscious, prerational emotional programming from childhood and our overidentification with a specific group or groups are the sources from which our false self—our injured, compensatory sense of who we are — gradually emerges and stabilizes. The influence of the false self extends into every aspect and activity of our lives, either consciously or unconsciously. Centering Prayer, and more particularly contemplative prayer for which it is a preparation, brings us face to face with this "false self" in several ways: The initial act of consent to letting go of our surface "I" with its programs, associations, commentaries, etc., in itself drives a fatal wedge into the false self. As we rest in prayer, we begin to discover that our identity is deeper than just the surface of our psychological awareness. (*IL*, 3)

Revelation 3:8 NJB

Look, I have opened in front of you a door
that no one will be able to close....

· May 2 ·

The "Divine Therapy"

Let us ... never stop trusting ... [Jesus].
Hebrews 4:14 NLT

The regular practice of contemplative prayer initiates a healing process that might be called the "divine therapy." The level of deep rest accessed during the prayer periods loosens up the hardpan around the emotional weeds stored in the unconscious, of which the body seems to be the warehouse. The psyche begins to evacuate spontaneously the undigested emotional material of a lifetime, opening up new space for self-knowledge, freedom of choice, and the discovery of the divine presence within. As a consequence, a growing trust in God, a bonding with the Divine Therapist, enables us to endure the process. (*IL*, 3)

Hebrews 4:14–16 NLT

Let us cling to ... [Jesus] and never stop trusting him. This High Priest of ours understands our weaknesses, for he faced all the same temptations we do, yet he did not sin. So let us come boldly to the throne of our gracious God. There we will receive his mercy, and we will find grace to help us when we need it.

· *May 3* ·

Moving Closer to God

Ah, the sheer grace! —
Saint John of the Cross

The gift of contemplative prayer is a practical and essential tool for confronting the heart of the Christian ascesis — namely, the struggle with our unconscious motivation — while at the same time establishing the climate and necessary dispositions for a deepening relationship with God and leading, if we persevere, to divine union. Meanwhile, the same process of letting go (of thoughts, feelings, commentaries, etc.), first experienced during the prayer period, becomes the basis for a practice of consent that can be carried into all of life, enabling us more and more to live the values of the gospel. (*IL*, 3–4)

Matthew 19:16, 20–21 NLT

Someone came to Jesus with this question: "Teacher, what good things must I do to have eternal life?...I've obeyed all...[the] commandments....What else must I do?" Jesus told him, "If you want to be perfect, go and sell all you have and give the money to the poor, and you will have treasure in heaven. Then come, follow me."

· *May 4* ·

Confrontation with the False Self

Show me the path...I should walk, O LORD....
Psalm 25:4 NLT

The biblical desert symbolizes the confrontation with the false self and interior purification. Jesus was tempted regarding each one of the instinctual needs. He did not consent to them while yet experiencing them in their utmost intensity — "He was tempted in every way that we are, yet never sinned" (Heb. 4:15)....Having rejected the exaggerated demands of each of the emotional programs for happiness, he invites us to do the same, saying, "Repent." This is as if he were to say, "Change the direction in which you are looking for happiness. You'll never find it in your emotional programs for happiness. Let go of your childish motivation because it can't possibly work in adult life." (*IL*, 11)

Nehemiah 9:19 NIV

Because of your great compassion you did not abandon them in the desert.

· May 5 ·

Divine Mercy

Mercy within mercy within mercy.
Thomas Merton

The experience of God's love and the experience of our weaknesses are correlative. These are the two poles that God works with as he gradually frees us from immature ways of relating to him. The experience of our desperate need for God's healing is the measure in which we experience his infinite mercy. The deeper the experience of God's mercy, the more compassion we will have for others. (*IL*, 17)

James 5:11 NIV

The Lord is full of compassion and mercy.

· *May 6* ·

Call to Transforming Union

Wash me . . . I will be whiter than snow.
Psalm 51:7 NLT

We learn to trust God beyond our psychological experiences. And we become more courageous in facing and letting go of the dark corners of ourselves and begin to participate actively in the dismantling of our pre-rational emotional programs. We cannot escape from the worldliness that is inside us, but we can acknowledge and confront it. The invitation to allow God to change our motivation from selfishness to divine love is the call to transforming union. (*IL*, 18)

Psalm 51:5–7 NLT

For I was born a sinner —
yes, from the moment my mother conceived me.
But you desire honesty from the heart,
so you can teach me to be wise in my inmost being.
Purify me from my sins, and I will be clean;
wash me, and I will be whiter than snow.

· *May 7* ·

Passive Purification of Contemplative Prayer

He purified their hearts by faith.
Acts 15:9 NIV

Not every method is adequate or sufficiently comprehensive to deal with the subtleties of the false self. We need to choose one that is suitable for our state of life. We may also require some psychotherapy. Regular periods of contemplative prayer are the keystone of the whole program; they need to be reinforced by positive efforts in daily life to change our inveterate habits of acting under the influence of the emotional programs for happiness. But having acknowledged the essential character of efforts to change, we must emphasize what Paul pointed out in the passage from Romans: The conscious resolution to change our values and behavior is not enough to alter the unconscious value systems of the false self and the behavior they engender. Only the passive purifications of contemplative prayer can effect this profound healing. Only then will the reservoir of interior silence, built up in periods of contemplative prayer, never run dry. (*IL*, 22–23)

Zechariah 4:6 NIV

"Not by might nor by power, but by my Spirit," says the LORD Almighty.

· May 8 ·

Afflictive Emotions

Live by the Spirit....
Galatians 5:16 NIV

Any upsetting emotion is warning us that an emotional program may just have been frustrated. The cause may not be somebody else's misconduct or an unpleasant event. For us to be habitually happy, nobody has to change except ourselves. If we are upset by anything, we have a problem, and we will continue to experience emotional turmoil until we change the root of the problem, which is the emotional program for happiness in the unconscious. The effort to change it is called the practice of virtue. If we keep our desires and aversions dried out by not watering them with commentaries or acting them out, they wither like weeds in the desert. (*IL*, 24)

Galatians 5:16–17 NIV

So I say, live by the Spirit, and you will not gratify the desires of the sinful nature. For the sinful nature desires what is contrary to the Spirit, and the Spirit what is contrary to the sinful nature. They are in conflict with each other, so that you do not do what you want.

· May 9 ·

Growth

God . . . gives to all generously. . . .
James 1:5 NAB

Every movement of human growth precipitates a crisis appropriate to the level of physical, emotional, or
spiritual development at which we find ourselves. Each
major crisis of growth requires letting go of the physical
or spiritual food that has been nourishing us up to then
and moving into more mature relationships. In such a
crisis we tend to seek the feeling of security. . . . The
capacity to go forward into personal responsibility is
constantly challenged. . . . Human growth is not the de-
nial or rejection of any level, but the integration of the
lower into more evolved levels of consciousness. . . . The
gospel calls for full the development of the human person and invites us to the further growth that God has
in store for us. . . . (*IL*, 30–31)

Isaiah 58:11 NAB

The LORD will guide you always and give you plenty
even on the parched land.

· *May 10* ·

Right Relationship with God

Holy and awesome is His name.
Psalm 111:9 NASB

One of the chief factors that tend to destroy relationships among people and nations is the emotion of fear.
It also destroys the relationship between us and God. To
be afraid of God, or to be afraid of other people, makes
us defensive. In the case of God, we will try to stay as
far away from him as our situations and the demands of
respectability permit. In the case of other people, we try
to control them and hold them within limits that enable
us to feel secure. The biblical term "fear of God" does
not refer to the emotion of fear. Fear of God is a technical term in the Bible meaning the right relationship with
God. The right relationship with God is to trust him.
The right relationship with God involves reverence and
awe for God's transcendence and immanence as well as
trust in his goodness and compassion. (*IL*, 37)

Psalm 111:4, 7, 9–10 NIV

The LORD is gracious and compassionate....
The works of his hands are faithful and just;
all his precepts are trustworthy....
holy and awesome is his name....
To him belongs eternal praise.

· *May 11* ·

Fallen Human Nature

Return to your rest, O my soul....
Psalm 116:7 NASB

As long as intimacy with God was enjoyed by our first parents, everything in creation was friendly. As soon as that intimacy was lost, briars grew up instead of crops and all the ills of fallen human nature came upon them. These images reflect what we experience in our own psychological awarenesses. We come to full reflective self-consciousness without the easy intimacy with God that Adam and Eve enjoyed in the garden. We lack a sense of oneness with God, other people, and the cosmos. We feel incomplete and afraid and hence seek symbols of security, affection, and power to shore up our fragile self-identities. When the gospel of John proclaims, "The word became flesh," the author is indicating that God took upon himself not human nature in its ideal state before the Fall, but human nature in its actual condition of privation, sin, and death. (*IL*, 41)

John 1:14 NASB

And the Word became flesh, and dwelt among us....

· *May 12* ·

Abundant Life Is Divine Union

[Jesus gives] ... life in all its fullness.
John 10:10 NLT

God often invites us to rethink the judgments we made in childhood and adolescence, or in the early years of our conversion, that amounted to a rejection of the goodness of his gifts. He invites us to take another look at our hesitations and to realize that our rigid attitudes were based on our inability to handle events and relationships that were emotionally traumatic. Now he asks us to accept the legitimate pleasures of life, the value of friendship, the exercise of our talents, the loveliness of nature, the beauty of art, the enjoyment of both activity and rest. God is a tremendous supporter of creation, especially of all living beings. Jesus emphasized this when he said, "I came that they might have life and have it to the full" (John 10:10). The abundant life is divine union, which includes the capacity to use all things as stepping stones to God rather than as ends in themselves. (*IL*, 48)

John 10:10 NLT

My purpose is to give life in all its fullness.

· May 13 ·

The True Self

Put aside your old self....
Ephesians 4:22 NJB

By consenting to God's creation, to our basic goodness as human beings, and to the letting go of what we love in this world, we are brought to the final surrender, which is to allow the false self to die and the true self to emerge. The true self might be described as our participation in the divine life manifesting in our uniqueness. God has more than one way of bringing us to this point. It can happen early in adult life, but if it does not, the ongoing stages of natural life may contribute to bringing it about. In the midlife crisis, even very successful people wonder whether they have accomplished anything. Later we experience physical decline, illness, and the infirmities of old age. What happens in the process of dying may be God's way of correcting all the mistakes we made and all the opportunities we missed during the earlier part of our lives. It may also provide the greatest chance of all to consent to God's gift of ourselves. (*IL*, 48–49)

2 Corinthians 9:15 NASB

Thanks be to God for His indescribable gift!

· May 14 ·

Dismantling the False Self

Be filled with love that comes from a pure heart. . . .
1 Timothy 1:5 NLT

[The biography of] Saint Anthony of Egypt, the fourth-century father of Christian monasticism, . . . provides a paradigm for dismantling the false self by means of both active confrontation and passive purification. [The life of Cistercian Brother Bernie O'Shea] . . . exemplifies the positive way of dismantling the false self by practicing unconditional love: selfishness cannot survive in the climate of continuous self-giving. A combination of the two ways may be the most practical response to the human condition. . . . Dismantling . . . [the false self] often feels like interior warfare — and in fact, it is! . . . Worldly temptations that kept pounding . . . [Anthony of Egypt] were not outside him, but inside him. . . . What was his method of resistance? Faith, determination, and incessant prayer. (*IL,* 58, 63)

2 Corinthians 7:1 NIV

Since we have these promises, dear friends, let us purify ourselves from everything that contaminates body and spirit, perfecting holiness out of reverence for God.

· *May 15* ·

Night of Sense

Now you are full of light from the Lord....
Ephesians 5:8 NLT

The night of sense, John of the Cross asserts, happens "fairly soon" to those who commit themselves to the spiritual journey. By the term *night* John of the Cross means the darkening of the usual ways in which we relate to God, whether through reflection or through the experience of the senses. Our ordinary ways of relating to God are being changed to ways that we do not know. This pulls the rug out from under our plans and strategies for the spiritual journey. We learn that the journey is a path that cannot be mapped out in advance. God helps us to disidentify from our preconceived ideas by enlightening us from within by the contemplative gifts of the Spirit. Through the infusion of his light and the assurance of his love, he lets us in on our weaknesses and deficiencies — not to overwhelm us with discouragement, but to encourage us to entrust ourselves completely to his infinite mercy. (*IL*, 69–70)

Ephesians 5:8 NLT

For though your hearts were once full of darkness, now you are full of light from the Lord, and your behavior should show it!

· May 16 ·

A Call into the Unknown

I will show you.... I will bless you....
Genesis 12:1–2 NLT

The spiritual journey is a call into the unknown. Its scriptural paradigm is the call of Abraham: "Leave your father's house, your friends, relatives, and property, and come into the land that I will show you" (Gen. 12:1). God first calls us out of our childish ways of reacting into relationships that are appropriate for full mental egoic consciousness [full emergence of moral responsibility for our behavior and relationships]. But after that has been stabilized, we have not the remotest idea where God is taking us. Paul says, "Eye has not seen, ear has not heard, nor has it so much as dawned on man what God has prepared for those who love him" (1 Cor. 2:9). The only way to get there is to consent not to know. The desire or demand for certitude is an obstacle to launching full sail on the ocean of trust. (*IL*, 75)

Genesis 12:1–2 NLT

Then the LORD told Abram, "Leave your country, your relatives, and your father's house, and go to the land that I will show you.... I will bless you...."

· *May 17* ·

The Gift of God's Infinite Mercy

> God ... in his ... mercy gave us a new birth. ...
> *1 Peter 1:3 NAB*

We cannot bring the false self to an end by ourselves; we can only allow it to die. If we do what we can to dismantle it, God, in response to our efforts, moves in and completes the job. All we have to do then is to consent. But that is about the biggest job there is. When all our efforts have failed, we finally accept the gift of God's infinite mercy. The night of sense enables us to perceive that the source of the emotional programs for happiness is selfishness. By letting go of our desires for satisfaction in these areas, we move toward a permanent disposition of peace. Upsetting thoughts and emotions arise, but they no longer build up into emotional binges. The immense energy that was required to bear the afflictive emotions that flared up when our programs for happiness were frustrated is now available for more useful things, such as loving the people with whom we live and whom we are trying to serve. (*IL*, 75–76)

1 Peter 1:3 NLT

All honor to the God and Father of our Lord Jesus Christ, for it is by his boundless mercy that God has given us the privilege of being born again.

· *May 18* ·

The Work of Purification

Lord, all Your ways are perfect.

God holds back his infinite mercy from rushing to the rescue when we are in temptation and difficulties. He will not actively intervene because the struggle is opening and preparing every recess of our being for the divine energy of grace. God is transforming us so that we can enjoy the divine life to the full once it has been established. If the divine help comes too soon, before the work of purification and healing has been accomplished, it may frustrate our ultimate ability to live the divine life. (*IL*, 81–82)

Psalm 27:14 NKJV

Wait on the LORD;
Be of good courage,
And He shall strengthen your heart;
Wait, I say, on the LORD!

· *May 19* ·

A Sense of God's Absence

I formed you . . . I shall not forget you.
Isaiah 44:21 NJB

The night of sense is about dismantling our immature programs for happiness, which can't possibly work in adult life. Little do we realize when we embark on the spiritual journey that our first fervor is itself immature and under the influence of these programs; it will have some growing up to do. Thus, at some point in our journey, a pervasive sense of God's absence begins to manifest itself during prayer and spreads into other areas of one's life. This is actually the beginning of a deeper union with Christ. Most of us, however, do not experience it that way. When the biblical desert opens up within us, we worry that something is going wrong in our relationship with God. (*IL*, 84)

Isaiah 44:21 NJB

Remember these things . . .
I formed you . . .
I shall not forget you.

· *May 20* ·

Death of the False Self

Put to death ... your old self. ...
Colossians 3:5, 9 NIV

The night of sense is designed to bring about the dismantling of the emotional programs and the death of the false self. The fruit of this purifying process is the freedom to decide what to do, without interference from the compulsions and fixations of the false self. It took constant effort to keep ourselves in some semblance of peace when we were seeking fantastic goals that were constantly frustrated, setting off the afflictive emotions of anger, grief, fear, pride, lust, greed, jealousy, and the other capital sins. As the false self diminishes and trust in God increases in the night of sense, our energies can be put to better purposes. (*IL*, 85)

Colossians 3:5, 9–10, 12 NIV

Put to death ... your old self with its practices and ... put on the new self, which is being renewed in knowledge in the image of its Creator. ... Clothe yourselves with compassion, kindness, humility, gentleness and patience.

· *May 21* ·

Deepening Our Relationship With God

You shall indeed find him....
Deuteronomy 4:29 NAB

The night of sense enables us to face our distorted views of God and to lay them aside. Then we are free to relate to God as he is and to use the immense energy that this freedom releases to relate to other people with respect and love. One way God deals with the limited ways we have of relating to him is by reducing our concepts of him to silence. As resting in God in contemplative prayer becomes habitual, we spontaneously disidentify with our emotional programs for happiness and our cultural conditioning. Already we are meeting God at a deeper level. In time we will grow from a reflective relationship with God to one of communion. The latter is a being-to-being, presence-to-presence relationship, which is the knowledge of God in pure faith. (*IL*, 87)

Deuteronomy 4:29 NAB

You shall seek the LORD, your God; and you shall indeed find him when you search after him with your whole heart and your whole soul.

· *May 22* ·

Commitment

[Jesus said], "Follow me."
Luke 5:27 KJV

The night of sense brings the nature of commitment into clear focus. When we take to heart Jesus' words, "Follow me," he invites us into his friendship. Friendship always involves commitment to the other person. This is the disposition that enabled Anthony [Saint Anthony of Egypt, the fourth-century father of Christian monasticism] to get through all his temptations and to reach transforming union. His basic means were always the same: commitment to the spiritual journey, the practice of constant prayer, and trust that God would give him the strength to persevere.... God is calling us in the night of sense to take responsibility for ourselves and for our personal response to Christ's invitation to follow him. (*IL*, 87, 89)

Ephesians 6:10–11, 16–18 NRSV

Be strong in the Lord and in the strength of his power. Put on the whole armor of God:... the shield of faith, ... the helmet of salvation, and the sword of the Spirit, which is the word of God. Pray in the Spirit at all times ... always persevere....

· May 23 ·

The Night of Spirit and the First Fruit

[God] gives grace to the humble.
Proverbs 3:34 NIV

As [you] have seen, the night of sense virtually im-
mobilizes the false self. Its residue, however, is still
lingering in our spiritual faculties and manifests itself
by the secret satisfaction that we find in ourselves as
the recipients of God's favors.... The night of spirit,
the beginning of divine union according to John of the
Cross, is a further transitional stage involving a more
intimate purification.... The night of spirit is designed
to free us from the residue of the false self in the
unconscious and thus to prepare us for transforming
union.... Without that purification, the consequences
of the false self are not completely erased.... The spiritual journey is not a success story, but a series of
diminutions of self.... The night of the spirit is an
intensive course in humility.... The first [fruit of the
night of spirit] ... purifies the secret satisfaction of being
chosen as the recipient of God's special gifts. (*IL*, 95–97)

Psalm 25:9 NIV

He guides the humble in what is right
and teaches them his way.

· May 24 ·

Second Fruit of the Night of Spirit

We are God's work of art....
Ephesians 2:10 NJB

A second fruit of the night of spirit is freedom from the domination of any emotion....This takes place not by repressing or unduly suppressing unwanted emotions by sheer willpower, but by accepting and integrating them into the rational and intuitive parts of our nature. The emotions will then serve and support the decisions of reason and will, which is their natural purpose. The integration of our emotional life with reason and faith and the subjection of our whole being to God constitute Saint Thomas Aquinas's definition of human happiness. In his view, human beings were meant to act in harmony with their nature and to enjoy doing so. This harmonious state is substantially restored in the night of spirit by extinguishing the last traces of our subjection to the emotional programs for happiness in the spiritual part of our nature. As for the emotional and sense levels, they were laid to rest in the night of sense. (*IL*, 97–98)

Ephesians 2:10 NJB

We are God's work of art, created in Christ Jesus for the good works which God has already designated to make up our way of life.

· May 25 ·

Third Fruit of the Night of Spirit

The awesome glory of the LORD....
Exodus 24:17 NLT

A third fruit of the night of spirit is the purification of our idea of God, the God of our childhood or the God worshipped by the particular group to which we belong.... God reveals himself in the night of spirit in a vastly superior way — as infinite, incomprehensible, and ineffable — the way that he appeared to Moses on Mount Sinai and to Elijah on Mount Horeb. No one can describe the experience of pure faith. We know only that an immense and unnameable energy is welling up inside. This immense energy may be experienced by some as impersonal, although it certainly treats us in a personal way. *(IL, 98)*

Exodus 24:16–17 NLT

And the glorious presence of the LORD rested upon Mount Sinai.... The awesome glory of the LORD on the mountaintop looked like a devouring fire.

· *May 26* ·

Fourth Fruit of the Night of Spirit

Say "I will" to all that God asks.
Jean-Pierre de Caussade

A fourth fruit of the night of spirit is the purification of what are traditionally known as the "theological virtues," which are faith, hope, and love. In the purification of faith...one allows God to be God without knowing who or what that is. Total self-surrender and abandonment grow mightily, though in a manner hidden from us, in the night of spirit. The divine light is so pure that it is imperceptible to any of our faculties. According to John of the Cross, pure faith is a ray of darkness....We simply trust in God's infinite mercy. Mercy of its nature reaches out to weakness and extreme need. We begin to be content with God's infinite mercy. Divine love is infused in the seedbed of total submission and self-surrender and brings us through the night of spirit into the transforming union. (*IL*, 98–99)

Genesis 28:16 NLT

Then Jacob woke up and said, "Surely the LORD is in this place, and I wasn't even aware of it."

· May 27 ·

Fifth Fruit of the Night of Spirit

Tenderly you swell my heart with love.
Saint John of the Cross

A fifth fruit of the night of spirit is the longing to let go of the selfishness that still lingers in us and to be free of every obstacle that might hinder our growth in divine union. According to John of the Cross, the same fire of divine love that is experienced painfully in the night of spirit becomes gentle and full of love in the transforming union. The "I" of self-centeredness diminishes to a very small "i." The great "I AM" of Exodus looms in its place. Thus, the divine plan is to transform human nature into the divine, not by giving it some special role or exceptional powers, but by enabling it to live ordinary life with extraordinary love. (*IL*, 99)

2 Corinthians 13:3, 5 NJB

His power is at work among you.... Do you not recognize yourselves as people in whom Jesus Christ is present?

· *May 28* ·

The Spirit Gives Us the Courage

Live...your new life in the...Spirit.
Galatians 5:16 NLT

While remaining grateful for the good things we have received and loyal to family and social group, we recognize that such loyalty is not an absolute. We try to improve unhealthy or unjust situations in our family or community instead of clinging to a naive loyalty that refuses to see defects or fails to suggest improvements or corrections that should be made. We have the freedom to remain within our tradition or institution, while at the same time working for its renewal. We do what we can to improve family, church, or social situations without demanding results or expecting to see the fruits of our labors. The Spirit gives us courage to make our personal response to Christ, rather than one that is based on what others say, do, or expect. (*IL*, 107)

Ephesians 4:23–25 NLT

There must be a spiritual renewal of your thoughts and attitudes. You must display a new nature because you are a new person, created in God's likeness — righteous, holy, and true. So put away all falsehood and "tell your neighbor the truth" because we belong to each other.

· May 29 ·

Surrender

Into your hands...I commend my soul....
Charles de Foucauld

The way of pure faith is to persevere in contemplative practice without worrying about where we are on the journey, and without comparing ourselves with others or judging others' gifts as better than ours. We can be spared all this nonsense if we surrender ourselves to the divine action, whatever the psychological content of our prayer may be. In pure faith, the results are often hidden even from those who are growing the most.... The divine light of faith is totally available in the degree that we consent and surrender ourselves to its presence and action within us. It heals the wounds of a lifetime and brings us to transforming union, empowering us to enter Christ's redemptive program, first by the healing of our own deep wounds, and then by sharing in the healing of others. (*IL*, 118–19)

2 Corinthians 1:3–4 NRSV

Blessed be...the Father of mercies and the God of all consolation, who consoles us in all our affliction, so that we may be able to console those who are in any affliction with the consolation with which we ourselves are consoled by God.

· *May 30* ·

From Contemplation to Action

Blessed are the peacemakers....
Matthew 5:9 NJB

More than any other institution, they [world religions]
have an obligation to address the problem of world
peace and to emphasize the human values that they
mutually share and proclaim. Their collective conscience could challenge the nationalistic interests of
world powers. But as yet they have no networking process or place where they might speak with one voice
on behalf of basic human values, especially justice and
peace. We cannot expect the military establishment to
end war. War is their profession. The only way that war
can be eliminated is to make it socially unacceptable.
If the world religions would speak to the human family regarding its common source and the potential of
every human being to be transformed into the divine, a
moral voice of great power would be introduced on behalf of the innocent and of the human family as a whole.
(*IL*, 124)

Matthew 5:9 NJB

Blessed are the peacemakers:
they shall be recognized as children of God.

· *May 31* ·

Spirituality in Everyday Life

Come....inherit the Kingdom....
Matthew 25:34 NLT

"Do I have to wait until I have been completely puri-fied before I can begin to serve others or practice the corporal works of mercy?" To this Jesus replies, "I was hungry and you gave me food, I was thirsty and you gave me drink. I was a stranger and you welcomed me" (Matt. 25:35). In the light of these words, the exercise of compassion does not sound like a big deal. It could mean giving someone a cup of water, a smile, or showing concern to someone suffering a loss. We do not have to wait until we can speak at the United Nations or go to Moscow for a summit conference. Somebody is in need right next door, in our family, at work, on the bus — everywhere we turn. (*IL*, 128–29)

Matthew 25:40 NLT

I assure you, when you did it to one of the least of these my brothers and sisters, you were doing it to me!

· June 1 ·

Focus of First Half of Spiritual Journey

Where are you? ... Why are you hiding?
Genesis 3:9 NRSV and TCLB

Where are you? This is one of the great questions of all time. It is the focus of the first half of the spiritual journey.... In Genesis 3 it is the question God asked when Adam and Eve had taken off for the underbrush after their disobedience.... This marvelous story of creation is not just about Adam and Eve. It is really about us. It is a revelation of where *we* are. The same question is addressed to every generation, time, and person. At every moment of our lives, God is asking us, "*Where* are you? Why are you hiding?" (*HC,* 7)

Genesis 3:8–9 NRSV

They heard the sound of the LORD God walking in the garden at the time of the evening breeze, and the man and his wife hid themselves from the presence of the LORD God among the trees of the garden. But the LORD God called to the man, and said to him, "Where are you?"

· June 2 ·

Beginning the Spiritual Search for God

With my whole heart I seek you....
Psalm 119:10 NRSV

All the questions that are fundamental to human happiness arise when we ask ourselves this excruciating question: *Where* am I? Where am I in relation to God, to myself, and to others? ... As soon as we answer honestly, we have begun the spiritual search for God, which is also the search for ourselves. God is asking us to face the reality of the human condition, to come out of the woods into the full light of intimacy with him. That is the state of mind that Adam and Eve had, according to the story, before their disobedience. As soon as they became aware of their separation from God, they headed for the woods. They had to hide from God because the loss of the intimacy and union that they had enjoyed with him in paradise was so painful. (*HC*, 7–8)

Psalm 119:10 NRSV

With my whole heart I seek you....

· June 3 ·

A Sufi Tale about the Human Condition

> They will seek my face....
> *Hosea 5:15 NIV*

A Sufi master had lost the key to his house and was look-ing for it in the grass outside.... [One of his] disciples said, "Master, have you any idea where you might have lost the key?" The Master replied, "Of course. I lost it in the house." To which they all exclaimed, "Then why are we looking for it out here?" He said, "Isn't it obvious? There is more light here."... The house in the para-ble represents happiness, and happiness is intimacy with God, the experience of God's loving presence.... This is the human condition — to be without the true source of happiness, which is the experience of the presence of God, and to have lost the key to happiness, which is the contemplative dimension of life.... What we experience is our desperate search for happiness where it cannot possibly be found. The key is not in the grass; it was not lost outside ourselves. It was lost inside ourselves. That is where we need to look for it. (*HC*, 8–10)

Hosea 5:15 NIV

> And they will seek my face;
> in their misery they will earnestly seek me.

· June 4 ·

Lost Intimacy with God

He alone is perfect happiness....
Saint Thérèse of Lisieux

Adam and Eve lost the intimacy they had enjoyed with God. God used to visit them in the cool of the evening. They had an easy relationship with him. As soon as they fell into a discriminating mind by eating of the tree of the knowledge of good and evil, they became self-conscious; they experienced themselves not only as separate from God but also, because of their sin, as alienated from God. Contemporary psychology has a significant contribution to make at this point.... [Self-consciousness] emerges gradually through various stages of a child's development. Full self-reflective consciousness begins around the ages of twelve to fourteen. Prior to that time, we have an innate thirst for happiness but no practical experience of the presence of the divine within us. So we look for happiness somewhere else. (*HC*, 10–11)

Isaiah 59:2 NIV

Your iniquities have separated you from your God; your sins have hidden his face from you....

· June 5 ·

Substitutes for the Divine Presence

Be on your guard against false gods.
1 John 5:20 NJB

All of us have been through the process of being born and entering this world with three essential biological needs: security and survival, power and control, affection and esteem. Without adequate fulfillment of these biological needs, we probably would not survive infancy. Since the experience of the presence of God is not there at the age we start to develop self-consciousness, these three instinctual needs are all we have with which to build a program for happiness. Without the help of reason to modify them, we build a universe with ourselves at the center. . . . As a result, any object entering into our universe — another person or event — is judged on the basis of whether it can provide us with what we believe or demand happiness to be. . . . In the Old Testament, substitutes for the divine presence were called . . . false gods. (*HC*, 13, 11)

Exodus 20:2–5 NIV

I am the LORD your God. . . . You shall have no other gods before me. You shall not make for yourself an idol in the form of anything. . . . You shall not bow down to them or worship them; for I, the LORD your God, am a jealous God. . . .

· June 6 ·

The Beginning of the Addictive Process

O God of compassion, heal my soul.

Children who are deprived of security, affection, and control needs develop a desperate drive to find more and more symbols of these basic human needs in their culture. This is called compensation. It can also happen that when experiences in early childhood are unbearable, they are repressed into the unconscious. The body seems to be a kind of warehouse in which all our experiences — the whole of our lives — are recorded. . . . Here, then, is the beginning of what might be called the addictive process, the need to hide the pain that we suffered in early life and cannot face. We repress it into the unconscious to provide an apparent freedom from the pain or develop compensatory processes to access forms of pleasure that offset the pain we are not yet prepared to face. (*HC*, 13–14)

Revelation 2:9 NRSV

I know your affliction and your poverty,
even though you are rich.

· June 7 ·

Homemade Self or False Self

The LORD knows our thoughts . . . are . . . empty breath.
Psalm 94:11 NRSV

We are thrust because of circumstances into the position
of developing a homemade self that does not conform to
reality. Everything entering into the world that makes
survival and security, affection and esteem, and power
and control our chief pursuits of happiness has to be
judged on the basis of one question: Is it good for *me?*
Hence, good and evil are judged not by their objective
reality, but by the way we perceive them as fitting into
our private universe or not. . . . The homemade self or
the false self, as it is usually called, is programmed for
human misery. (*HC*, 14–15)

Romans 3:16–17 NIV

[As it is written:] "Ruin and misery mark their ways, and
the way of peace they do not know."

· June 8 ·

Looking for Happiness in Wrong Places

For God alone my soul waits in silence....
Psalm 62:5 NRSV

The combination of . . . two forces — the drive for happiness in the form of security and survival, affection and esteem, and power and control, and overidentification with the particular group to which we belong — greatly complicates our emotional programs for happiness. In our younger days, this development is normal. As adults, activity arising from such motivation is childish. . . . Without facing . . . early childhood excesses and trying to dismantle or moderate them, . . . they continue to exert enormous influence throughout life. . . . The distortion of human nature becomes habitual and is supported, like the Sufi master's disciples, by others who are doing the same thing — trying to find happiness where it cannot possibly be found. (*HC*, 15–16)

Psalm 62:5 NRSV

For God alone my soul waits in silence,
for my hope is from him.

· *June 9* ·

Which Way toward Happiness?

Repent and believe the good news!
Mark 1:15 NIV

When Jesus said, "Repent," to his first disciples, he was calling them to change the direction in which they were looking for happiness. "Repent" is an invitation to grow up and become a fully mature human being who integrates the biological needs with the rational level of consciousness. The rational level of consciousness is the door that swings into higher states — the intuitive and unitive levels of consciousness. They open us to the experience of God's presence, which restores the sense of happiness. We can then take possession of everything that was good in our early life while leaving the distortions behind. (*HC*, 17)

Matthew 4:17 NIV

Repent, for the kingdom of heaven is near.

· June 10 ·

Conversion

Cleanse me from my unknown faults.
Psalm 19:13 NAB

Conversion addresses the heart of the problem. Jesus
has some harsh sayings that are incomprehensible unless
we see them in the light of the harm that our emotional
programs are doing. For example, Jesus said, "If your
foot scandalizes you, cut it off." He wasn't recommend-
ing self-mutilation but was saying that if your emotional
programs are so close to you that you love them as much
as your own hand or foot or eye, get rid of them. They
are programs for human misery that will never work.
They will interfere with all your relationships — with
God, yourself, other people, the earth, and the cosmos.
(*HC*, 18)

Psalm 19:13 NAB

Who can detect heedless failings?
Cleanse me from my unknown faults.

· *June 11* ·

Consequences of Unconscious Motivation

> I do not understand my own actions.
> *Romans 7:15 NRSV*

All the emotional programs for happiness, overidentification with one's group, and the commentaries that reinforce our innate tendencies have sources in the unconscious as well as in the conscious. That is why St. Paul could say, "What I want to do, I don't do. And what I don't want to do I find myself doing" (Rom. 7:15ff.). If we don't face the consequences of unconscious motivation — through a practice or discipline that opens us to the unconscious — then that motivation will secretly influence our decisions all through our lives. (*HC*, 18–19)

Romans 7:15 NRSV

I do not understand my own actions. For I do not do what I want, but I do the very thing I hate.

· *June 12* ·

Willingness to Be Exposed to the Unconscious

My way is all of trust and love.
Saint Thérèse of Lisieux

One needs a willingness to be exposed to the unconscious. This requires some courage and persistence. We can't call up the unconscious at will. With the help of psychotherapy, we might be able to call up some of it. The dark nights described by St. John of the Cross go much deeper. Normally, emotions need to be expressed in some way in order to be processed. Emotions are energy. If they are not processed, they become blocks in our bodies and nervous systems to the free flow of our energy systems and of grace. When we are not thinking, analyzing, or planning and place ourselves in the presence of God in faith, we open ourselves to the contents of the unconscious. (*HC*, 19)

Matthew 14:27 NLT

Jesus spoke to them.... "It's all right," he said. "I am here! Don't be afraid."

· June 13 ·

Daily Practice of Contemplative Prayer

Help me, Lord, to persevere.

What matters most is fidelity to the daily practice of a contemplative form of prayer such as Centering Prayer. This gradually exposes us to the unconscious at a rate that we can handle and places us under the guidance of the Holy Spirit. Divine love then prepares us to receive the maximum that God can possibly communicate of his inner light. Besides the dark side of the unconscious, there are all kinds of other awesome energies — for example, natural talents, the fruits of the Spirit, the seven gifts of the Spirit, and the divine indwelling itself — that we haven't experienced yet and that are waiting to be discovered. (*HC*, 20)

Hebrews 10:36 NIV

You need to persevere so that when you have done the will of God, you will receive what he has promised.

· June 14 ·

True Humility

With humility comes wisdom.
Proverbs 11:2 NIV

The contemplative journey, because it involves the purification of the unconscious, is not a magic carpet to bliss. It is an exercise of letting go of the false self, a humbling process, because it is the only self we know. God approaches us from many different perspectives: illness, misfortune, bankruptcy, divorce proceedings, rejection, inner trials. God has not promised to take away our trials, but to help us to change our attitudes toward them. That is what holiness really is. In this life, happiness is rooted in our basic attitude toward reality. Sometimes a sense of failure is a great means to true humility, which is what God most looks for in us. (*HC*, 20–21)

Matthew 11:29 NJB

Learn from me, for I am gentle and humble in heart....

· *June 15* ·

Transformation of Our Inmost Being

I will make darkness light before them....
Isaiah 42:16 NKJV

The false self is looking for fame, power, wealth, and prestige. The unconscious is very powerful until the divine light of the Holy Spirit penetrates to its depths and reveals its dynamics. Here is where the great teaching of the dark nights of St. John of the Cross corresponds to depth psychology, only the work of the Holy Spirit goes far deeper. Instead of trying to free us from what interferes with our ordinary human life, the Spirit calls us to transformation of our inmost being, and indeed of all our faculties, into the divine way of being and acting. (*HC*, 22)

2 Corinthians 3:18 NIV

We ... are being transformed into his likeness with ever-increasing glory, which comes from the Lord, who is the Spirit.

· June 16 ·

Take Responsibility for Being Human

Now is the time to seek the LORD....
Hosea 10:12 NLT

God invites us to take responsibility for being human
and to open ourselves to the unconscious damage that
is influencing our decisions and relationships. If psy-
chologists and psychiatrists would be in dialogue with
the insights of St. John of the Cross and those who experience the dark nights, there could be a marvelous
symbiosis of treatment. We are not sick just because of
some physiological pathology. It is not just a question
of sin either; it is a question of the human condition,
for which none of us is initially responsible but, on
becoming adults, we are now called to be responsible.
(*HC*, 24)

Hosea 10:12 NLT

Plant the good seeds of righteousness, and you will harvest a crop of my love. Plow up the hard ground of your
hearts, for now is the time to seek the LORD, that he may
come and shower righteousness upon you.

· June 17 ·

Friendship with God

You are my friends.... I chose you.
John 15:15–16 NLT

How do we cultivate any friendship? By spending
time together with those to whom we are attracted.
There are stages of building any relationship, beginning with getting acquainted, which is a bit awkward;
through friendliness, which is more pleasant; to friendship, which is a commitment; to various levels of union
and unity that restore the state of intimacy that was lost
symbolically in the Garden of Eden. Here we are under
the influence of unconscious drives of various intensity
that in turn influence our decisions and relationships
with other people and foul them up.... Contemplative
prayer is a deepening of faith that moves beyond
thoughts and concepts. One just listens to God, open
and receptive to the divine presence in one's inmost
being as its source. One listens not with a view to hearing something, but with a view to becoming aware of
the obstacles to one's friendship with God. (*HC*, 24–25)

Isaiah 57:14 NASB

Remove every obstacle out of the way of My people.

· June 18 ·

Painful Repressed Memories

God...called you...into his...light.
1 Peter 2:9 NIV

Contemplative prayer starts modestly, but as soon as it begins to reach a certain intensity, it opens us to the unconscious. Painful memories that we have forgotten or repressed begin to come to consciousness. Primitive emotions that we felt as children and that we have been compensating for may come to consciousness. How should we handle these afflictive emotions? By facing them, by feeling them. Feelings that have been repressed have to be allowed to pass through our awareness once again in order to be left behind for good. Most of the time, they don't need psychotherapy; they just need to be evacuated. (*HC*, 25)

1 Peter 2:9–10 NIV

God...called you out of darkness into his wonderful light....now you are the people of God...now you have received mercy.

· *June 19* ·

Contemplative Prayer
Heals the Whole Person

The LORD will answer:..."Here I am."
Isaiah 58:9 THS

Some problems, admittedly, are so serious that one needs psychiatric help. It is important that there be teamwork between spiritual guides and psychological professionals. If we are talking about the health of a human being, we are not just talking about the body or even the emotions; we are talking about the whole range of human potential, including spiritual health. These all have to be treated at once if we want to get well. This is what contemplative prayer does. But it doesn't act alone. Its fruits need to be worked into daily life. (*HC*, 26)

Isaiah 58:8–9 THS

Then shall thy light break forth as the morning,
And thy healing shall spring forth speedily....
Then shalt thou call, and the LORD will answer;
Thou shalt cry, and He will say: "Here I am."

· June 20 ·

The Divine Therapy

In Your Presence, Lord, I am healed.

The Gospel introduces us to the divine therapy for the illness of the human condition in the form of contemplative prayer, which addresses not only the distortions of our conscious behavior, but also the dynamics of the unconscious. . . . The divine therapy, like Alcoholics Anonymous, is based on the realization that you know where you are and that your life is unmanageable. We may be able to lead a relatively normal life, but there is no experience of the true happiness that comes from letting go of the obstacles to the awareness of the divine presence. . . . Unless our selfish programs for happiness have begun to be dismantled by a spiritual practice or discipline, we are not aware that events and people or our plans and memories are dominating our awareness from morning to night. (*HC*, 28, 31)

Romans 8:5–6 NLT

Those who are dominated by the sinful nature think about sinful things, but those who are controlled by the Holy Spirit think about things that please the Spirit. If your sinful nature controls your mind, there is death. But if the Holy Spirit controls your mind, there is life and peace.

· June 21 ·

The Presence of God Is True Security

Be silent, and know that I am God!
Psalm 46:10 NLT

Suppose that through a practice like Centering Prayer, which prepares us for contemplation, the primary locus of the divine therapy, we take half an hour every day for solitude and silence, just to be with God and with ourselves (without knowing yet who that is). As a result of the deep rest and silence that come through such a practice, our emotional programs begin to be relativized. They were designed at a time when we didn't know the goodness and the reassurance of God's presence. The presence of God is true security. There really isn't any other. (*HC*, 31–32)

Psalm 46:1 NLT

God is our refuge and strength,
always ready to help in times of trouble.

· June 22 ·

True Freedom

Listen to me in silence. . . .
Isaiah 41:1 NRSV

Through a spiritual practice like Centering Prayer, we begin to experience spiritual awareness. Ordinary life then becomes like a lousy movie where we don't identify with the characters or plot. We can get up and leave — something we can't do in daily life when we overidentify with our ordinary stream of awareness and its contents. That is the inner tyranny that opposes true freedom. The freedom of the children of God means we can *decide* what to do about particular events. We live more and more out of self-actuating motivation rather than the domination of our habitual drives to be esteemed, to be in control, to feel secure. (*HC*, 32)

2 Corinthians 3:17 NIV

Now the Lord is Spirit, and where the Spirit of the Lord is, there is freedom.

· June 23 ·

Rest That Is Deeper Than Sleep

Listen! my beloved is knocking.
Song of Solomon 5:2 NRSV

Once a regular practice of Centering Prayer has been established, we move normally in each period of prayer toward a place of rest where our faculties are relatively calm and quiet. Thoughts are coming downstream, but as we learn to disregard them, we begin to enjoy a sense of the divine presence. Beyond our thinking and emotional experience is the deeper reality of the spiritual level of our being. It is another way of knowing reality that is unlike ordinary psychological awareness. As a result, not only is the mind quiet and at rest from the ordinary concerns of daily life, but the body also begins to rest, a rest that is deeper than sleep. (*HC*, 33–34)

Song of Solomon 5:2 NRSV

I slept, but my heart was awake.
Listen! my beloved is knocking.
"Open to me ... my love ... my perfect one. ..."

· *June 24* ·

The Divine Therapy

I have seen their ways, but I will heal them....
Isaiah 57:18 NRSV

The paradox is that we can never fully fulfill our role until we are ready to let it go. Whoever we think we are, we are not. We have to find that out, and the best way to do so, or at least the most painless way, is through the process that we call the spiritual journey. This requires facing the dark side of our personality and the emotional investment we have made in false programs for happiness and in our particular cultural conditioning. Rest in Centering Prayer provides us with profound healing. To be really healed requires that we allow our dark side to come to full consciousness and then to let it go and give it to God. The divine therapy is an agreement that we make with God. We recognize that our own ideas of happiness are not going to work, and we turn our lives over completely to God. (*HC*, 35)

Isaiah 57:18 NRSV

I have seen their ways, but I will heal them;
I will lead them and repay them with comfort....

· June 25 ·

Submit to the Divine Therapy

Work in us what is pleasing to ... [You].
Hebrews 13:21 NIV

To submit to the divine therapy is something we owe to ourselves and the rest of humanity. If we don't allow the Spirit of God to address the deep levels of our attachments to ourselves and to our programs for happiness, we will pour into the world the negative elements of our self-centeredness, adding to the conflicts and social disasters that come from overidentifying with the biases and prejudices of our particular culture and upbringing. This is becoming more important as we move into a global culture and into the increasing pluralism of religious beliefs. (*HC*, 36)

Hebrews 13:20–21 NIV

May the God of peace ... equip you with everything good for doing his will, and may he work in us what is pleasing to him, through Jesus Christ, to whom be glory for ever and ever. Amen.

· June 26 ·

Grow Up!

Accept one another....
Romans 15:7 NIV

What are we going to do when we are surrounded with people whose belief systems are quite different from our own? Where will our support come from? Instead of finding support that will back up our own belief system, we might look more profitably for the self-differentiation that enables us to be fully ourselves, with the acceptance of our limitations. As we become more aware of the dynamics of our unconscious, we can receive people and events as they are, rather than filtered through what we would like them to be, expect them to be, or demand them to be. This requires letting go of the attachments, aversions, "shoulds," and demands on others and on life that reflect the mentality of a child rather than that of a grownup. (*HC*, 36–37)

Romans 15:7 NIV

Accept one another...just as Christ accepted you....

· *June 27* ·

Evil and Humility

Deliver us from evil....
Matthew 6:13 KJV

None of us knows until we have been through difficult problems and tragedies what we would do in a challenging situation. Once I attended a panel discussion of people who had suffered during the Holocaust and other barbaric oppressions of this century. One woman on the panel had survived the Holocaust, but her parents had been killed. She had started a humanitarian organization to prevent such horrors from being repeated and mentioned casually, "You know, I couldn't have started that organization unless I knew that, with the situation just a little different, I could have done the same things that the Nazis did to my parents and the others in the concentration camps." This woman, it seems to me, possessed true humility — the knowledge of one's self that clearly perceives that with just a little change of circumstances, one is capable of any evil. (*HC*, 37–38)

Matthew 6:13 KJV

And lead us not into temptation, but deliver us from evil: For thine is the kingdom, and the power, and the glory, for ever. Amen.

· June 28 ·

Hanging in When God Seems Distant

How long, O LORD, how long?
Psalm 6:3 NIV

Our agreement with the divine therapist is to allow the Holy Spirit to bring us to the truth about ourselves. This initial period of conversion corresponds to the spring-time of the spiritual life, when prayer is easy, and we have great energy in pursuing...various forms...of so-cial service. As we begin to trust God more, we enjoy a certain freedom from our vices and may often experi-ence great satisfaction in our spiritual endeavors. When God decides we are ready, he invites us to a new level of self-knowledge. God withdraws the initial consolations of conversion, and we are plunged in darkness, spiritual dryness, and confusion. We think that God has aban-doned us.... Then comes a period of peace, enjoyment of a new inner freedom, the wonder of new insights. That takes time. Rarely is there a sudden movement to a new level of awareness that is permanent. What happens when we get to the bottom of the pile of our emotional debris? We are in divine union. There is no other obstacle. (*HC*, 39, 42)

Romans 4:20 NLT

Abraham never wavered in believing God's promise. In fact, his faith grew stronger, and in this he brought glory to God.

· June 29 ·

Who Are You?

He must increase, but I must decrease.
John 3:30 KJV

As long as we are identified with some role or persona, we are not free to manifest the purity of God's presence. Part of life is a process of dropping whatever role, however worthy, you identify with. It is not you. Your emotions are not you. Your body is not you. If you are not those things, who are you?...The ultimate abandonment of one's role is not to have a self as a fixed point of reference; it is the freedom to manifest God through one's own uniqueness....To be no one is to be everyone. To be no self is to be the true Self. To be nothing is to be everything. In a sense, it is to be God. For Christians, it is to be a kind of fifth Gospel: to become the word of God and to manifest God rather than the false self, with its emotional programs for happiness and attachments to various roles, including the most spiritual. When you have been liberated from them all, you are in a space that is both empty of self and full of God....If we have not experienced ourselves as unconditional love, we have more work to do, because that is who we really are. (*HC,* 42, 44, 45)

John 3:30 KJV

He must increase, but I must decrease.

· June 30 ·

Humiliation of the False Self

God ... gives grace to the humble.
1 Peter 5:5 NASB

Every movement toward the humiliation of the false self, if we accept it, is a step toward interior freedom and inner resurrection. This new freedom is not control; it is the freedom not to demand of life whatever we used to feel was essential for our particular *idea* of happiness. The divine therapy is an extraordinary project. Only God could have thought it up, and only God can persuade people to do it. I don't say that this will necessarily happen to everyone. But we are offered the opportunity. The priority we give to the invitation is up to us. (*HC*, 42–43)

1 Peter 5:5–6 NASB

God ... gives grace to the humble. Therefore humble yourselves under the mighty hand of God, that He may exalt you at the proper time. ...

· July 1 ·

Divine Indwelling

God lives in us....
1 John 4:12 NIV

The start, middle, and end of the spiritual journey is the conviction that God is always present. As we progress in this journey, we perceive God's presence more and more. As we emerge from childhood into full, reflective self-consciousness, our concept of how God is present in us is usually vague and primitive. The spiritual journey is a gradual process of enlarging our emotional, mental, and physical relationship with the divine reality that is present in us but not ordinarily accessible to our emotions or concepts.... The fundamental theological principle of the spiritual journey is the Divine Indwelling. The Trinity is present within us as the source of our being on every level. (*FG*, 2–3)

1 John 4:12 NIV

No one has ever seen God; but if we love one another, God lives in us and his love is made complete in us.

· July 2 ·

In the Silence of Our Hearts

[Maranatha]...Come, Lord Jesus.
Revelation 22:20 KJV

Our prayer, as contemplative persons, is the constant exercise of faith, hope, and charity (Divine Love), and takes place in the silence of our hearts as we listen to the Word of God — not just with our ears or minds, but with our inmost being. God speaks best by silence. This does not mean that we do not have unwanted thoughts during prayer, but that we return again and again to the basic consent of self-surrender and trust. We say "yes" to that presence, and every now and again enter into union with it as we identify the divine presence in Christ's humanity with the divine presence within us. When we say, "Come, Lord Jesus," we should remember that Christ is already here and that his coming means that he becomes more and more present to our consciousness. (*FG*, 10–11)

John 1:38–39 NJB

Jesus turned round, saw them following and said, "What do you want?" They answered, "Rabbi" — which means Teacher — "where do you live?" He replied, "Come and see."...

· July 3 ·

Purification and Contemplative Prayer

The Spirit...intercedes for us....
Romans 8:26 NIV

I often use the example of the spiral staircase as a symbol of the purification that gradually takes place through contemplative prayer. In doing this I mean to suggest that every time we move to a new level of recognition of our weakness and dependence on God for everything, we experience a kind of inner resurrection. To put it in terms of the Twelve Steps of Alcoholics Anonymous, the more we realize how "unmanageable" our lives are — how helpless we are to practice the virtues and to imitate Jesus — the more life becomes an adventure in allowing the Spirit to move us and to accompany us in daily life. (*FG,* 14)

Romans 8:26–27 NIV

The Spirit helps us in our weakness.... The Spirit... intercedes for us.... And he who searches our hearts knows the mind of the Spirit, because the Spirit intercedes...in accordance with God's will.

· July 4 ·

Fruits and Gifts of the Spirit

The Holy Spirit gives life.
2 Corinthians 3:6 NLT

The Spirit is present to our inmost being all the time, inviting us to let go of our self-centered projects and to allow the Spirit to be the source of our actions at every level. With that kind of trustful dependence on the Spirit, each time we accept a new sense of our own weakness and lack of virtue there follows an inner resurrection. This is manifested by the experience of the Fruits of the Spirit. The Fruits are the first indication of our transformation in Christ. As we descend the spiral staircase into the depths of our own being and into the center of our nothingness, the Seven Gifts of the Spirit, which are even more mature fruits, begin to manifest themselves. (*FG*, 14–15)

John 11:25 NLT

Jesus said:
I am the resurrection and the life.

· July 5 ·

The Presence of the Spirit

Let us . . . follow the Spirit.
Galatians 5:25 NAB

The Spirit is present within us by virtue of our Baptism, when we were anointed with the Spirit. Unfortunately, when we are not available to the Spirit, we think that the Spirit is absent. The power of the Spirit is intensified in the sacrament of Confirmation, when the Seven Gifts of the Spirit are explicitly transmitted to us. Our unconscious contains all the emotional trauma of a lifetime (that we have repressed) as well as enormous levels of energy and creativity. Every significant event of our life history is recorded in our bodies and nervous system. The undigested emotional material of a lifetime must be moved out in order for the free flow of grace and the natural and spiritual energies in the unconscious to manifest themselves. These energies appear as the qualities of charity, joy, peace, kindness, generosity, faithfulness, gentleness, and self-control. (*FG*, 15)

Galatians 5:22–23, 25 NAB

The fruit of the Spirit is love, joy, peace, patience, kindness, generosity, faithfulness, gentleness, self-control. . . . If we live in the Spirit, let us also follow the Spirit.

· July 6 ·

First Fruit of the Spirit: Charity

He will be silent in His love....
Zephaniah 3:17 THS

The first Fruit of the Spirit is *Charity* or, in the Greek, Agape, which means self-giving love as opposed to self-seeking love. Most of us know love as desiring something or someone. This is the kind of love the Greeks called Eros, a powerful and necessary kind of love but one that is meant to grow into the self-giving love that the Gospel calls charity. Charity is not almsgiving. It is rather a participation in God's unconditional love.... The growth of charity leads to self-surrender to God and to the compassionate love of others. The quality of Christ's love is the source of its vitality; the continual tender and loving awareness of the presence of God is its reward.... Where does this charity come from? It is being infused into us in the silent seedbed of contemplative prayer. (*FG*, 16–18)

Romans 5:5 NRSV

God's love has been poured into our hearts through the Holy Spirit that has been given to us.

· July 7 ·

Second Fruit of the Spirit: Joy

The joy of the LORD is your strength.
Nehemiah 8:10 NIV

The second Fruit of the Spirit is *Joy*. Joy is an abiding sense of well-being based on the experience of a conscious relationship with God. It is the sign of liberation from the false self and the growing awareness of the true self. Flowing from joy comes the freedom to accept the present moment and its content without trying to change it. Bliss might be described as the fullness of joy. It is the abiding sense of being loved by God and of being permanently established in his presence. It is the experience of the living water that flows from the divine Source in our inmost being, which Jesus spoke about in John's Gospel. (*FG*, 18)

John 7:37–39 NIV

Jesus stood and said in a loud voice, "If anyone is thirsty, let him come to me and drink. Whoever believes in me, as the Scripture has said, streams of living water will flow from within him." By this he meant the Spirit, whom those who believed in him were later to receive.

· July 8 ·

Third Fruit of the Spirit: Peace

My peace I give you.
John 14:27 NIV

The third Fruit of the Spirit is *Peace*. Peace is the pervasive sense of contentment that comes from being rooted in God while being fully aware of one's own nothingness. It is a state that endures beyond the ups and downs of life, beyond the emotions of joy and sorrow. At the deepest level one knows that all is well, that everything is just right despite all appearances to the contrary. At all times one can pray with Jesus, "Father, into your hands I commend my spirit" (Luke 23:46). (*FG, 19*)

Philippians 4:7 NIV

And the peace of God, which transcends all understanding, will guard your hearts and your minds in Christ Jesus.

· July 9 ·

Fourth Fruit of the Spirit: Meekness

Make me Resemble you, Jesus!
Saint Thérèse of Lisieux

The fourth Fruit of the Spirit is *Meekness* (kindness). Meekness is freedom from the energy of hostility, hatred, or outbursts of anger. Anger is necessary for human health and growth. But it needs to be transmuted into a growing capacity to persevere in the pursuit of the difficult good, especially the immense goods of the spiritual journey and of the imitation of Christ. The growth of meekness opens us to the continual awareness of God's presence and the acceptance of everyone with their limitations. One does not approve of the harmful things that others may do, but one accepts them as they are and is ready to help whenever possible — but without trying to change them. One is even content with one's inability to change oneself as one would like while continuing to do what one can to improve, relying more and more upon God and less and less on one's own efforts. (*FG*, 19–20)

Matthew 5:1–2, 5 *NIV*

His disciples came to him, and he began to teach them, saying: ... Blessed are the meek, for they will inherit the earth.

· *July 10* ·

Fifth Fruit of the Spirit: Faithfulness

All for thee, sweet Jesus.
Prayer from childhood

The fifth Fruit of the Spirit is *Faithfulness* (fidelity). Faithfulness is the dynamic expression of meekness. It is the daily oblation of ourselves and all our actions to God out of compassion for others, especially in service of their concrete needs. It serves God without dwelling on what God or others will do for us, and perseveres in giving without thinking of any return. Our normal need for affirmation is coming from a new place: the growing conviction of being loved by God that greatly reduces the desire for human approval. (*FG*, 20)

1 Corinthians 16:14 NJB

Let everything you do be done in love.

· July 11 ·

Sixth Fruit of the Spirit: Gentleness

Help me to learn God's gentle Way.

The sixth Fruit of the Spirit is *Gentleness*. Gentleness is a participation in God's way of doing things that is at once gentle and firm, sustaining all creation with its enormous diversity, yet without effort. We labor in the service of God more than ever, and yet have the sense of stepping back and watching God make things happen according to his will both in ourselves and in others. Our anxious efforts to serve God and our anguished search for God cease. Like God we labor and are at rest at the same time. We work hard but we know by experience, even by bitter experience, that our efforts are not going to go anywhere except insofar as God makes them fruitful. Hence vanity, jealousy, and contention — which often accompany even our spiritual endeavors — are gradually evacuated, leaving immense freedom just to be who we are and to serve the special needs of those around us. (*FG*, 20–21)

Matthew 11:29 NJB

Learn from me, for I am gentle and humble in heart. . . .

· *July 12* ·

Seventh Fruit of the Spirit: Goodness

Everything God...created is good....
1 Timothy 4:4 NJB

The seventh Fruit of the Spirit is *Goodness*. Goodness is the affirmation of creation as good, together with a sense of oneness with the universe and with everything created. It is the disposition that perceives events, even the tragic things of life, as manifestations of God's love. It recognizes the beauty of all creation in spite of the damage that human selfishness has imposed upon it. As a result, gratitude to God abounds in our hearts and a positive attitude characterizes our relationship with others and with the wear and tear of daily life. (*FG*, 21)

Psalm 27:13 NLT

I am confident that I will see the LORD's goodness while I am here in the land of the living.

· July 13 ·

Eighth Fruit of the Spirit: Patience

Ask and it will be given to you....
Matthew 7:7 NAB

The eighth Fruit of the Spirit is *Long-suffering* (patience). Long-suffering is certitude in God's unwavering fidelity to his promises. Our security is no longer based on anything we might possess or accomplish, but rather on our conviction of God's unfailing protection and readiness to forgive. Hence we are not easily disturbed by the ebb and flow of human events and our emotional reactions to them. Feelings continue to be felt, at times more strongly than ever, but they no longer dominate our awareness or our activity. We are content to wait with confidence for God's deliverance in every situation, especially during prolonged periods of dryness and the dark nights. We have interiorized the words of the Gospel: "Ask and you shall receive. Seek and you shall find. Knock and the door shall be opened to you" (Matt. 7:7). (*FG*, 21–22)

Matthew 7:7 NAB

Ask and it will be given to you; seek and you will find; knock and the door will be opened to you.

· *July 14* ·

Ninth Fruit of the Spirit: Self-Control

[God's] steadfast love ... never ceases. ...
Lamentations 3:22 NRSV

The ninth Fruit of the Spirit is *Self-control.* Self-control as a fruit of the Spirit is not the domination of our will over our emotions. It is rather our awareness of God's abiding presence and is the result of the infusion of God's steadfast love. Hence our former compulsive reaching out for security, affection and esteem, power and status symbols ceases. In particular, there is no energy for sexual activity apart from commitment and genuine love. When Moses asked God who he was, the answer came: "I AM THAT I AM." This text is still under scholarly investigation, but one likely meaning is "I am *for* you." The inward assurance of God's unwavering love enhances our freedom of choice and action. Out of that interior liberty, self-control arises spontaneously. We know in spite of our weakness that God will give us the strength to get through every trial and temptation. (*FG*, 22–23)

Lamentations 3:22 NRSV

The steadfast love of the LORD never ceases,
his mercies never come to an end. ...

· *July 15* ·

The Seven Gifts of the Spirit

I welcome Faith, Hope, and Divine Love.

The Seven Gifts of the Spirit...are acts and movements of the Spirit that purify and raise us to a divine mode of knowledge through the growth of the theological virtues of Faith, Hope, and Charity (Divine Love), which are the transforming virtues in the Christian scheme of things. Isaiah 11:2 lists these gifts as Wisdom and Understanding, Counsel and Fortitude, Knowledge,...Fear of the Lord,...[and] Piety. The Holy Spirit, through the Gifts, is especially our guide in the practice of Centering Prayer and in accompanying programs to bring its effects into daily life. The presence of the Holy Spirit within us is always inviting us to listen to the delicate inspirations that gradually take over more and more aspects of our lives, and to transform them from expressions of our false self into manifestations of our true self and of the infinite goodness and tenderness of the Father. (*FG*, 26)

Ephesians 4:24 NIV

Put on the new self, created to be like God in true righteousness and holiness.

· July 16 ·

Pleading for the Supreme Gift of the Spirit

You send forth Your Spirit....
Psalm 104:30 NASB

What are you really doing when you sit down in Centering Prayer and open yourself to God's presence and action within you? You are opening to God's presence and consenting to God's activity. God's activity is the work of the Holy Spirit in your particular embodiment in this world.... We are pleading for the supreme gift of the Spirit simply by consenting to God's will and action. (*FG*, 28)

Psalm 104:30 NIV

When you send your Spirit, they are created,
and you renew the face of the earth.

· *July 17* ·

Abba Isaac's Commentary

Fill me with Your Holy Spirit.

Abba Isaac, one of the Desert Fathers and member of a fourth-century lay contemplative movement . . . explains . . . "We pray with the door shut when, without opening our mouths and in perfect silence, we offer our petitions to the One who pays no attention to words, but looks hard at our hearts." In other words, God looks at our intention much more than our attention. In Centering Prayer our basic disposition is "Fill me with your Holy Spirit, the supreme Gift, according to your promise. I don't know how to ask rightly, so I sit here waiting, asking you to pray in me, asking for what you most want to bestow, your Holy Spirit." (*FG*, 29, 31)

Matthew 6:6 NRSV

Whenever you pray, go into your room and shut the door and pray to your Father who is in secret. . . .

· July 18 ·

Cultivating Our Spiritual Level

Love is repaid by love alone.
Saint Thérèse of Lisieux

It is our hearts that we are offering to God in Centering Prayer, hearts that are pleading for the Holy Spirit
and, at the same time, putting up with the weakness of
human nature and our own personal melodrama, for the
love of God. As we return to the sacred symbol again
and again, we gradually become aware that we are cultivating the spiritual level of our awareness. In this sense,
every time we move from a thought into the place of
interior silence we are renewing our love for God. We
do not judge our prayer by how many thoughts we have,
however much we are bombarded by them. Rather, we
judge it by how promptly we go back *ever so gently* to
our sacred symbol. Thus we may have made hundreds
of acts of the love of God in the course of a single period of Centering Prayer! The Gifts of the Holy Spirit
grow in direct proportion to the depth and sincerity of
our love. (*FG*, 35)

Luke 24:32 NRSV

Were not our hearts burning within us
while he was talking to us...?

· *July 19* ·

Consent to God's Presence

Our Father . . . Your will be done. . . .
Matthew 6:9–10 NASB

If we emphasize what God is doing for us, as we do in Centering Prayer, we start the spiritual journey from a different place than has been traditional in the past. We begin the journey not with ourselves and what we are going to do for God, but with God and what God is doing for us. We consent to God's presence, letting God decide what he wants us to do. God seems to want to find out what it is like to live human life in us, and each of us is the only person who can ever give him that joy. Hence our dignity is incomparable. We are invited to give God the chance to experience God in our humanity, in our difficulties, in our weaknesses, in our addictions, in our sins. Jesus chose to be part of everyone's life experience, whatever that is, and to raise everyone up to divine union. (*FG*, 42)

Acts 17:28 NRSV

In him we live and move and have our being. . . .

· July 20 ·

Gift of Reverence

God's truth ... lives in us. ...
2 John 1:1–2 NLT

The Gift of Reverence keeps us true to ourselves and to God. It tells the truth in love and will not back down for motives of self-defense or security. Reverence is not only the fear of offending God prompted by love, but it is loyalty to one's own personal integrity: to do what one believes is right no matter what the stakes are. ... As the Gift of Reverence grows stronger, our trust in God expands. Humility is a profound sense of our weakness and nothingness, but at the same time an even greater trust in God's infinite mercy and compassion. The Gift of Reverence puts together these apparent opposites. (FG, 47–48)

1 Timothy 1:15–16 NLT

Christ Jesus came into the world to save sinners — and I was the worst of them all. But that is why God had mercy on me, so that Christ Jesus could use me as a prime example of his great patience with even the worst sinners.

· *July 21* ·

Gift of Fortitude

I am with you always....
Matthew 28:20 NJB

The Gift of Fortitude...gives energy to overcome major obstacles in the way of spiritual growth....The Spirit shows us how to sanctify our role in life so that we remain in the divine presence. This is why methods of remaining in God's presence are so valuable and necessary if we are seriously pursuing the spiritual journey....Little by little, the Gift of Fortitude, in conjunction with the other Gifts, transmutes the energy of anger designed by nature for defensive purposes into zeal for the service of God and the needs of others. It sustains difficult ministries and welcomes the vicissitudes of daily life instead of fighting or resisting them or giving way to feelings of frustration. It establishes a certain firmness of mind and heart in doing good and enduring evil, especially when these are difficult. It manifests its inspiration in the Beatitude: "Blessed are those who hunger and thirst after justice, for they shall be satisfied" (Matt. 5:6). (*FG*, 49–50, 56)

Romans 12:11 NJB

In the service of the Lord, work not halfheartedly but with conscientiousness and an eager spirit.

· July 22 ·

The Gift of Piety

Forgive as the Lord forgave you.
Colossians 3:13 NIV

The Gift of Piety mellows the sense of reverence for God and over-strictness with ourselves. It inspires a great spirit of kindness and understanding toward others, meekness in bearing their faults, willingness to forgive, and genuine affection for them. The Gift of Piety awakens in us a child-like attitude toward God and also a sense that everyone is our brother and sister. It sees people as companions on the journey rather than competitors. ...[An]...attitude of total forgiveness of everyone and everything is the most mature fruit of the Gift of Piety. As the sense of belonging to the human family as a whole continues to grow through contemplative prayer and practice, this oneness extends to the earth, the environment and, indeed, to all creation. One begins to perceive all things in God and God in all things. (*FG*, 57, 60)

Ephesians 4:32 NIV

Be kind and compassionate to one another, forgiving each other, just as in Christ God forgave you.

· July 23 ·

The Gift of Counsel

The Counselor . . . will teach you all things. . . .
John 14:26 NIV

The Gift of Counsel . . . not only suggests what to do
in the long range, but also what to do in the details of
our daily lives. The more open we are to the Spirit, the
more the Spirit takes over our lives. . . . Three stages frequently occur in action that is prompted by the Spirit.
The first is that you feel called by God to do something
that requires great effort, and sometimes the project
is initially a huge success. The next stage is that your
initial success fails. You feel that you made a mistake
and are humiliated. You resolve never to take a similar
risk. Finally, there is the triumph of grace, often totally unexpected. Those three elements almost always
go together. . . . All you have to do is to take the first
step. (*FG*, 63, 68)

Psalm 73:23–24 NRSV

You hold my right hand.
You guide me with your counsel. . . .

· July 24 ·

A Peaceful Inclination

The Spirit . . . will guide you to all truth.
John 16:13 NAB

The Gift of Counsel is a peaceful inclination to continue to do what we are doing or to change what we are doing. We can ignore it. It is a suggestion. Take it or leave it. To develop that sensitivity requires work on our part to maintain interior silence, but once it is established the only time we have to take action is when we notice a loss of peace. That means that we are off course. As long as that peace is in place, we are in deep prayer all the time, whether we are praying formally or not. Whether we are counseling or doing heavy manual work, as long as that sense of inner quiet and peace is there, God is not asking us to think about or to judge the situation. He merely wants us to stay on course, to do his will in the present moment. (*FG*, 71–72)

Romans 12:2 NAB

Be transformed by the renewal of your mind, that you may discern what is the will of God, what is good and pleasing and perfect.

· July 25 ·

The Gift of Knowledge and Reality

Your face, LORD, do I seek.
Psalm 27:8 NRSV

There is a certain humbling character that the Gift
of Knowledge imparts — namely that we are basically
prone to illusion and that our way of looking at life is not
the only way and certainly not the most accurate. Such
knowledge opens us, like the opening of mind and heart
that we pursue in Centering Prayer, to the reality of God
just as God is.... The Gift of Knowledge is an intuition
into the fact that only God can satisfy our deepest longing for happiness.... The Spirit of God in response to
our Centering Prayer practice provides perspective for
the energy that is channeled into... [the] daily frustration of our immoderate desires. The Spirit says to us:
"You will never find happiness in any of your instinctual
needs. They are only created things, and created things
are designed to be stepping-stones to God, and not substitutes for God." The Spirit presents us with the true
source of happiness, which is the experience of God as
intimate and always present. (*FG*, 73–75)

Psalm 27:8 NRSV

"Come," my heart says, "seek his face!"

· July 26 ·

The Gift of Knowledge and Mourning

Blessed are they who mourn....
Matthew 5:4 NAB

The Gift of Knowledge corresponds to the beatitude of those who mourn. The reason we mourn is that something inside us realizes that our programs for happiness, put together in early childhood, are not going to work anymore. This is one of the intuitive fruits of the Gift of Knowledge. It is the realization of the damage that the emotional programs have done to us throughout our lives up until now. Part of the mourning caused by the Gift of Knowledge is the beautiful grace called "tears of contrition." Such contrition is also known as compunction. Compunction is the humble acknowledgement of our failures without any guilt feelings attached to them. If there are guilt feelings attached to them, then they are coming from our own neuroses. When there is a feeling of loving sorrow for having damaged ourselves and others, these tears are cleansing. Hence the promise contained in the beatitude: "Blessed are those who mourn, for they shall be comforted." (*FG*, 76–77)

Matthew 5:4 NAB

Blessed are they who mourn,
for they will be comforted.

· July 27 ·

The Gift of Knowledge and Purification

He satisfies the longing soul....
Psalm 107:9 NKJV

The exercise of Seven Gifts of the Spirit called the Beatitudes are the inner resurrections that take place as a result of the purification and humiliation of the false self. Perhaps the initial Gift that we come in contact with in the practice of Centering Prayer is the Gift of Knowledge, which is the knowledge of creatures in relation to God. This knowledge is precisely what we do not have as we emerge from our childhood with our various ways of coping with traumatic experiences. The Gift of Knowledge impresses upon us intuitively (that is, not through the reasoning process but intuitively as the fruit of prayer) that only God can satisfy. Usually this does not come as a sudden revelation but as a result of the gradual diminishing of our emotional programs for happiness and over-identification with our cultural conditioning.... The Spirit comes to our aid to the degree that we sincerely give ourselves to God and make ourselves compliant to the Divine Therapist. (*FG*, 78–80)

Psalm 17:15 NKJV

I shall be satisfied when I awake in Your likeness.

· *July 28* ·

Gift of Understanding: Truths of Faith

Jesus, thank You for Your light.

The Gift of Understanding reveals what is hidden in the major truths of Christian doctrine. The Gift of Understanding perfects, deepens, and illumines faith as to the meaning of revealed truth, adding new depths to the mystery to which we consent. For instance, it could be some aspect of the Holy Trinity or the greatness of God. It could be the presence of Jesus Christ in the Eucharist. It could be the infinite mercy of God in the Sacrament of Reconciliation. In other words, it is not merely the affirmation of something we believe and assent to. A characteristic of the Gift of Understanding is that it provides a kind of living experience of the mystery. One or two of those experiences can last a lifetime and make such a deep impression as to reorient one's whole spiritual life once and for all. (*FG*, 88)

1 Corinthians 2:10, 12 NRSV

These things God has revealed to us through the Spirit; for the Spirit searches everything, even the depths of God.... We have received... the Spirit that is from God, so that we may understand the gifts bestowed on us by God.

[209]

· July 29 ·

Gift of Understanding:
View Our Own Weakness

Let Your mercy shine upon evil. . . .
Saint Teresa of Avila

The Gift of Understanding . . . gives us a penetrating insight into the truths of faith and at the same time a realistic view of our own weakness. . . . It communicates the experience of our nothingness and our incapacity to do anything good by ourselves. . . . The Gift of Understanding, whether it comes through terrible suffering or develops gradually through a life of prayer, makes us aware that we are capable of any evil and that only God is our strength. Only God can protect us from the evil we might do if we were placed in circumstances of enormous tragedy and suffering. In this sharp light there can be no elation or pride in one's own gifts. There is no appropriation of one's own talents. . . . All of this is burned away . . . as we realize ever more profoundly that we owe infinitely more to God and to others than we can ever give back. Humility is the right relationship to God. It is at the same time total dependence on God and invincible hope in God's infinite mercy. (*FG*, 97, 101–2)

Matthew 5:8 KJV

Blessed are the pure in heart: for they will see God.

· *July 30* ·

Gift of Wisdom: The Divine Perspective

Christ ... the ... wonderful wisdom of God.
1 Corinthians 1:24 NLT

The Gift of Wisdom provides us God's view of things, a kind of divine perspective on reality that penetrates through events and perceives the divine presence and action at work, even in very tragic and painful situations. To see God in suffering is indeed a high level of the Gift of Wisdom. Some things are to be learned in this perspective that cannot be learned in any other way. The Gift of Wisdom is the source of the Beatitude of the Peacemakers, those who have established peace within themselves and who have ordered their own great variety of faculties into a unity that submits to God's direction and inspiration. They are also able to establish peace around them — whether it be in their families, communities, or the workplace. (*FG*, 107–8)

Matthew 5:9 NAB

Blessed are the peacemakers,
    for they will be called children of God.

· *July 31* ·

Gift of Wisdom: Centering Prayer

O taste and see that the LORD is good....
Psalm 34:8 NRSV

Is it really possible to taste God? The answer is yes, but we cannot bring it about by our own efforts. We can only prepare ourselves for it by reducing the obvious obstacles we can perceive and by allowing the action of divine love to purify our unconscious motivation. The Gift of Wisdom has a very important place in Centering Prayer because it is this gift that causes the prayer at times to be full of insights, delightful, and profoundly silent — a silence that can almost be tasted or heard. The Gift of Wisdom communicates the mystery of God's presence as a personal experience. It brings to an end any doubts about God's love for us that we might have brought with us from early childhood, such as feelings of rejection or lack of self-worth. There is no greater affirmation of our goodness than to be affirmed by the Divine Presence. (*FG*, 108)

Acts 2:28 NJB

You have taught me the way of life,
you will fill me with joy in your presence.

· *August 1* ·

Desire for Interior Silence

He restores my soul. . . .
Psalm 23:3 NKJV

Have you ever experienced a few moments of interior silence? How would you describe it? Is there not a sense of a very deep, all-pervading peace, a sense of well-being, and a delicate joy, all at once? Why is it such a difficult state to maintain or return to? It seems easier to forget about the whole experience than to be plagued by the pain of lingering outside a door that seems to be locked from the inside. Yet, in spite of this lingering pain, the repeated experience of interior silence is a need that everyone has in order to be fully human. Our capacity for the transcendent is precisely what distinguishes us most from the rest of visible creation. It is what makes us most human. (*HW,* 7)

Psalm 23:1–3 NKJV

The LORD is my shepherd;
I shall not want.
He makes me to lie down in green pastures;
He leads me beside the still waters.
He restores my soul. . . .

· *August 2* ·

Cultivate Interior Silence

Lord, from my heart flows living water.

The principal means monks use to cultivate interior silence — external silence, a certain measure of solitude, and a non-possessive attitude — can be put into a concentrated form, like a *capsule*, to be taken daily, or several times a day. The traditional word for this is contemplative prayer.... Contemplative prayer allows the hunger and thirst for God to well up. "On the last and great day of the Feast, Jesus stood up in the Temple and cried out with a loud voice: 'If any man thirst, let him come to me and drink. Out of his inmost being will flow rivers of living water. This he said of the Holy Spirit who was to be given to those who believe'" (John 7:37–38). By these words, we are urgently invited to put aside our preoccupations and come to Christ in the depth of our being. This movement and the experience which results from it are the basis for every genuine form of Christian spirituality. (*HW,* 10)

John 7:37–39 NRSV

[Jesus] cried out, "Let anyone who is thirsty come to me, and let the one who believes in me drink. As the scripture has said, 'Out of the believer's heart shall flow rivers of living water.'" Now he said this about the Spirit....

· August 3 ·

Christian Spirituality

Come away... and rest a while.
Mark 6:31 NAB

Every Christian, by virtue of the grace of baptism, *has* the vocation to oneness with the Father through Jesus Christ in the Holy Spirit. Everyone needs some kind of practice in order to accomplish this vocation. Obviously, a rule of life cannot be as detailed for those living in the world as it is for people in a monastery. But everyone has to build his or her own kind of enclosure as far as one's duties allow, by setting aside a certain amount of time every day for prayer and spiritual reading. Also, perhaps, one may dedicate a day every month, and a week every year, to being alone with the Lord. Jesus himself encouraged this in the Gospel when he said to the apostles,... (*HW*, 12)

Mark 6:31 NAB

Come away by yourselves to a deserted place and rest a while.

· *August 4* ·

Divine Love

Love each other.... as I have loved you....
John 13:34 NLT

Vulnerability means to be hurt over and over again without seeking to love less, but more. Divine love is sheer vulnerability — sheer openness to giving. Hence, when it enters the world, either in the person of Jesus or in one of his disciples, it is certain to encounter persecution — death many times over. But it will also encounter the joy of ever rising again.... Being vulnerable means loving one another as Christ loved us. If we did not have to forgive people, we would have no way of manifesting God's forgiveness toward us. People who injure us are doing us a great favor because they are providing us with the opportunity of passing on the mercy that we have received. By showing mercy, we increase the mercy we receive. The best way to receive divine love is to give it away, and the more we pass on, the more we increase our capacity to receive. (*HW,* 14–15)

John 13:34 NLT

I am giving you a new commandment: Love each other. Just as I have loved you, you should love each other.

· August 5 ·

Oneness of the Human Family

Jesus, . . . who is my neighbour?
Luke 10:29 KJV

Paul, in developing the idea of the human body as an image of the Mystical Body of Christ, wrote, "If one member suffers, all suffer together" (1 Cor. 12:26). The organic oneness of the human family achieved still greater unity by being incorporated into God's Son through his incarnation and resurrection. This oneness of the human family is an aspect of the mystery of Christ that needs strong emphasis today. It cuts across the differences of race, creed, color, or nationality. It requires us to respect religious and cultural differences rather than oppose them. Moreover, these differences are often complementary when properly understood, and point to the cosmic Christ. The gospel parable of the Good Samaritan means that our neighbor is anyone at all — anywhere — who is in need. In the Old Testament we are told, . . . (*HW,* 15)

Isaiah 58:7 NLT

I want you to share your food with the hungry and to welcome poor wanderers into your homes. Give clothes to those who need them, and do not hide from relatives who need your help.

· *August 6* ·

The Challenge of Sacrifice

You must be born again.
John 3:7 NLT

When divine love overflows from the interior life of the Trinity into our hearts, it immediately confronts our false selves, and we experience conflict. A struggle arises between this pure goodness — sheer giving — and the ingrained possessiveness, aggressiveness, and self-seeking which are so characteristic of us in our present condition. Thus, at the very heart of life is the challenge of sacrifice; of dying to our present condition in order to move to a higher level of life. This can only happen by letting go of the false self. Suffering and death are not enemies, but doors leading to new levels of knowledge and of love. Unless we are willing to sacrifice what we have now, we cannot grow. We grow by dying and rising again; by dying to where we are now and being reborn at a new level. (*HW,* 19)

John 3:5–7 NLT

Jesus replied, "The truth is, no one can enter the Kingdom of God without being born of water and the Spirit. Humans can reproduce only human life, but the Holy Spirit gives new life from heaven. So don't be surprised at my statement that you must be born again...."

· *August* 7 ·

Empty Out the False Self

Lover, Creator, Healer shine through.

When we work to surrender our own desires, world view, self-image, and all that goes to make up the false self, we are truly participating in Christ's emptying of himself, as Paul described it. We are emptying ourselves of the false self so that our true self, which is the Christ-life in us, may express itself in and through our human faculties. And we can do this because he handed over his human life to the Father, and at the same time he handed over the Divine Spirit to the human family. Jesus said, "If anyone would come after me, let him deny himself and take up his cross and follow me" (Matt. 16:24). What is this "self"? It is our thoughts, feelings, self-image, and world view. Jesus added, "Whoever would save his life will lose it, and whoever loses his life for my sake, will find it" (Matt. 16:25). That is, he will find eternal life, the Christ-life, welling up within. (*HW*, 22)

Matthew 16:24–25 NJB

If anyone wants to be a follower of mine, let him renounce himself and take up his cross and follow me. Anyone who wants to save his life will lose it; but anyone who loses his life for my sake will find it.

· *August 8* ·

Sharing in the Divine Life

Your heart shall swell with joy....
Isaiah 60:5 NKJV

Jesus... is fully human, body, soul and spirit. And yet we believe, as Christians, that this is the Son of God. Without confusion of his divine and human natures, he is the absolute in human form. Perhaps we can understand Jesus' identity as the Son of God more clearly by thinking of him in terms of the revelation of the Trinity. That revelation affirms what the mystics of all religions have intuited: that the ultimate nature of infinite being is love. God, the ultimate reality, the absolute, in a way beyond our comprehension, is a community of persons. As the Father has life in himself and pours it into his Son, and they rejoice in it together in the procession of the Holy Spirit, so the Son who has life in himself, shares the divine life with the whole human family through the outpouring of the Holy Spirit, and invites everyone to the banquet of eternal life. (*HW,* 28)

Isaiah 60:5 NKJV

Then you shall see and become radiant,
And your heart shall swell with joy....

· *August 9* ·

Divine Presence

His right hand doth embrace me.
Song of Solomon 2:6 KJV

"He who has seen me," Jesus said, "has seen the Father" (John 14:9). The Word of God was always present beyond time. In the incarnation, he became present *in* time. He enfolds us, therefore, both within the temporal sphere and beyond it, at one and the same time. As the bride in the Song of Solomon said, "His left hand is under my head and his right hand ready to embrace me" (Song of Sol. 2:6). His left hand signifies the dimension of time and his right hand the dimension of eternity. With the two arms of his human and divine natures, he enfolds us in the mystery of the incarnation in an incredibly strong embrace. (*HW*, 28)

Song of Solomon 2:6 KJV

His left hand is under my head,
and his right hand doth embrace me.

· *August 10* ·

Our Home in the Bosom of the Father

I am the Alpha and ... Omega....
Revelation 21:6 NLT

There are those who know Christ beyond time as "the
true light that enlightens everyone" (John 1:9). We must
bring them the good news of Christ *inside* of time, so
that all true seekers of God may experience his full
embrace. However, we Christians must not cling too
closely to the Christ *inside* of time. Rather, we must
allow him to bring us to the knowledge of himself *beyond*
time. We must know Jesus, not only in his beginning,
but in his end, not only in the crib, but in his ascension.
For we too have come from the bosom of the Father and
must find our home there. Christ in his divine being is
present in your heart, in mine, and in that of everyone,
waiting to be resurrected there, so that he can share with
us the divine life and love that circulates eternally in the
Trinity. (*HW*, 28–29)

Revelation 21:6 NLT

I am the Alpha and the Omega — the Beginning and
the End. To all who are thirsty I will give the springs of
the water of life without charge!

· *August 11* ·

Transformation into the Mind of Christ

Christ . . . to be known, loved . . . imitated. . . .
John Paul II

Paul says, "While we live, we are always being given up
to death for Jesus' sake, so that the life of Jesus may
be manifested in our mortal flesh" (2 Cor. 4:11). Thus,
according to his view, the passion and resurrection of
Christ are going on all the time. They are always present
and not limited to an historical moment. It was rather an
historical moment which introduced the eternal values
of the cross and resurrection into the whole of time. We
participate in Christ's divine life through baptism and
the other sacraments. As a consequence, we must learn
how to express the risen life of Jesus rather than our
false selves in our conduct and relationships. To attain
this union involves the transformation of our inmost
being and all our faculties into the mind of Christ. This
is the very fullness of salvation. The chief expression
of the mind of Christ is found in the classical text of
Philippians. . . . (*HW,* 33)

Philippians 2:5, 7–8 NRSV

Let the same mind be in you that was in Christ Jesus . . .
emptied . . . humbled . . . obedient. . . .

· *August 12* ·

Spiritual Maturity

Each part...helps the other parts grow....
Ephesians 4:16 NLT

Salvation is an on-going process of growth.... The Kingdom of God, Jesus said, "is like a grain of mustard seed" (Mark 4:31), the tiniest of seeds. The first stage of the process is to put the mustard seed into the ground where it germinates. Afterwards, it pushes a shoot through the earth and starts to grow. Later, it puts forth branches and leaves and becomes a tree. It is only at the end of the process, and not without a certain amount of pruning, that the tree bears fruit, and we observe with satisfaction that the seed has at last become something worthwhile. In similar fashion, the process of salvation is going on all the time, and although, for a Christian, it starts with faith in Jesus Christ and repentance, it has to go through a long period of growth before the follower of Christ becomes mature and "equipped for every good work" (2 Tim. 3:17). (*HW*, 35–36)

Ephesians 4:16 NLT

As each part [of the body of Christ] does its own special work, it helps the other parts grow, so that the whole body is healthy and growing and full of love.

· *August 13* ·

Salvation and Grace

The Word . . . gives light to everyone. . . .
John 1:9 NJB

Paul says that anyone who truly seeks God, believing
that God will reward him, will receive the gift of grace.
In other words, when anyone follows his conscience, in
which the law of God is written, at some point he will
meet the grace of Christ, since it is offered to everyone
of good will. Whether he knows the historical Jesus or
not, he will come to know Christ as the eternal Word
of God, the Cosmic Christ, who "enlightens everyone"
(John 1:9) and through whom "all things were made"
(John 1:3). He will come to know the Christ who is in
the inmost conscience of every man and woman, waiting to manifest himself to them in the degree that they
follow the promptings of their conscience. Whoever
attains to grace, attains the grace of Christ. (*HW,* 37)

John 1:3 NJB

Through him all things came into being,
not one thing came into being except through him.

· *August 14* ·

Christ's Death Restored Intimacy with God

Thank You, Jesus, for Your awesome gift.

The great gift which Christ won through his sacrificial death is intimacy and oneness with the Father. On the day of his resurrection he said triumphantly to Mary Magdalene, "Go to my brethren and say to them that I am ascending to my Father and *your* Father" (John 20:17). That is the great good news! The experience of intimacy with God, symbolized in Genesis by God's daily walk with Adam and Eve in the evening air (Gen. 3:8), is now available once again to the whole human family. The gates of heaven closing after Adam and Eve is a vivid symbol of the ripe fruits of original sin, which are man's alienation from God and from himself. Adam and Eve lost what they were intended to have, namely, intimacy with God, which is the only true source of security. (*HW*, 37–38)

John 20:17 NJB

I am ascending to my Father and your Father,
to my God and your God.

· *August 15* ·

Faith Matures

The LORD turns my darkness into light.
2 Samuel 22:29 *NIV*

Christian faith is a leap into the unknown. Experience confirms the wisdom of every act of trust. The alternation of the darkness of faith leading to understanding, and understanding illuminating the darkness of faith is the normal way that leads to the growth of faith. Like everyone else, God wants to be accepted as he is — and he happens to be infinite, incomprehensible, inexpressible. We have to accept him, then, in the darkness of faith. It is only when we can accept God as he is that we can give up the desire for spiritual experiences that we can feel. Faith is mature when we are at ease without particular experiences of God, when his presence is obvious without our having to reflect on it. One who has this faith simply opens his eyes and, wherever he looks, finds God. (*HW,* 40–41)

2 Samuel 22:29 *NIV*

You are my lamp, O LORD;
the LORD turns my darkness into light.

· *August 16* ·

Strengthen Faith

All things work together for good....
Romans 8:28 NRSV

Faith is strengthened by reading and meditation on the Word of God, prayer, fidelity to the duties of our state of life, and the acceptance of the circumstances of life. We must try to perceive Christ in the interruption of our plans and in the disappointment of our expectations; in difficulties, contradictions, and trials. No matter what happens, "We know that in everything God works for good with those who love him" (Rom. 8:28). The Holy Spirit works on our evolution not only by purifying and enlightening us from within, but also by allowing difficulties, trials, and temptations to assail us from without. This much is certain, that once we make up our minds to seek God, he is already seeking us much more eagerly, and he is not going to let anything happen to prevent his purpose. He will bring people and events into our lives, and...they are designed for the evolution of his life in us. (*HW,* 41)

Romans 8:28 NRSV

We know that all things work together for good for those who love God....

· *August 17* ·

Listen Eagerly to the Word of God

Listen, that you may have life.
Isaiah 55:3 NAB

The fruitfulness of *lectio divina* presupposes a certain calmness of mind when we come to it.... By reading a few pages of scripture, a few paragraphs, or perhaps only a few words, we find ourselves in the presence of God, our Father, our friend — this extraordinary person we are trying to know. We need to listen eagerly to his words, applying our whole being to them. This is the reason why the ancient custom was to read aloud, or at least to form the words on one's lips, so that the body, too, entered into the process. The Holy Spirit inspired those who wrote the scriptures. He is also in our hearts inspiring us and teaching us how to read and listen. When these two inspirations fuse, we really understand what scripture is saying; or at least we understand what God at this moment is saying to us through it. (*HW*, 46–47)

Luke 24:32 NAB

Were not our hearts burning [within us] while he spoke to us on the way and opened the scriptures to us?

· *August 18* ·

Lectio Divina

I am the bread of life.
John 6:35 NJB

Each period of *lectio divina* follows the same plan: reflection on the Word of God, followed by free expression of the spontaneous feelings that arise in our hearts. The whole gamut of human response to truth, beauty, goodness, and love is possible. As the heart reaches out in longing for God, it begins to penetrate the words of the sacred text. Mind and heart are united and rest in the presence of Christ. *Lectio divina* is a way of meditation that leads naturally to spontaneous prayer, and little by little, to moments of contemplation — to insights into the Word of God and the deeper meaning and significance of the truths of faith. This activity enables us to be nourished by the "bread of life" (John 6:35), and indeed to *become* the Word of God (John 6:48–51). (*HW,* 48)

John 6:48, 51 NJB

I am the bread of life....the living bread which has come down from heaven. Anyone who eats this bread will live forever....

· *August 19* ·

Find Him in the Silent Love
of Self-Surrender

The language He best hears is silent love.
Saint John of the Cross

Paul exhorts us to take for granted that we have already received as a pure gift in baptism all that we need in order to attain salvation by virtue of Christ's passion, death, and resurrection. We have only to enter by faith into the kingdom that has already been established in the depth of our spirit and take possession of it. Thus, if we truly give ourselves to God in faith and open our minds and hearts to him, we may begin to find him in the silence of the prayer of faith very quickly. The prayer of faith is an approach to God without concepts. It is to accept God as he is, in the way he presents himself to us in the scripture, impossible to contain in any concept, but not impossible to contact through the love of self-surrender. By means of the regular practice of the prayer of faith, the vestibule to contemplative prayer is gradually established. It is in that silence that the infused virtues and gifts of the Spirit are greatly strengthened and developed. (*HW,* 52)

Habakkuk 2:20 NIV

The LORD is in his holy temple;
let all the earth be silent before him.

· *August 20* ·

Prayer

Prayer is the laying aside of thoughts.
Evagrius

Prayer can be expressed in words, thoughts, or acts of the will. But fundamentally it is a movement of our spiritual nature; that is, of our intellect beyond thoughts and of our will beyond particular acts — at least beyond explicit acts. This movement toward God can be extremely subtle and delicate. The more simple it is, the more effective it is. It can be a wordless turning or opening of our awareness to God, whom we know is present. We do not have to conceptualize *how* he is present, because we really do not know. When as Christians, we enter into deep interior silence and our thoughts are "laid aside," as Evagrius puts it, and we have gone beyond the imagination and its working, where are we? It seems the only place we can possibly be is in our spirit; and since Christ dwells at the center of our spirit, we, as baptized Christians, may be coming closer to experiencing him, even without explicitly intending it. (*HW*, 57)

Ephesians 3:17 NIV

Christ . . . [dwells] in your hearts through faith.

· *August 21* ·

God Dwells at the Center of Our Being

> We are . . . the temple of . . . God.
> *2 Corinthians 6:16 NJB*

We may begin to be aware that God, the Word made flesh, is dwelling at the very center of our being. In any case, the movement toward interior silence triggers a phenomenon that might be called centering. St. John of the Cross . . . says that we are attracted to God as to our center, like a stone toward the center of the earth. If we remove the obstacles, the ego-self with all its paraphernalia, and surrender to God, we penetrate through the various layers of our psyche until we reach the very center or core of our being. At that point there remains one more center to which we may advance. This center is the Trinity, Father, Son, and Holy Spirit, who dwell at the inmost center of our being. It is out of that Presence that our whole being emerges at every moment. To be at this center is eternal life. To remain at this center in the midst of activity is what Christ called the reign of God. (*HW,* 58)

2 Corinthians 6:16 NJB

We are . . . the temple of the living God.
We have God's word for it. . . .

· *August 22* ·

The Common Heart of the World

The Spirit is the heart of the world.

One of the things that prayer, as it deepens, will affect is our intuition of the oneness of the human race, and, indeed, the oneness of all creation. As one moves into his own inmost being, he comes into contact with what is the inmost being of everyone else. Although each of us retains his own unique personhood, we are necessarily associated with the God-man, who has taken the whole human family to himself in such a way as to be the inmost reality of each individual member of it. And so, when one is praying in the spirit, in his inmost being, one is praying, so to speak, in everybody else's spirit. (*HW,* 64)

Wisdom 12:1 *NAB*

Your imperishable spirit is in all things!

· *August 23* ·

Christ Is at the Heart of all Creation

I will pour out my Spirit on all....
Joel 2:28 NIV

In the Eucharist, we are not only joined to Christ, whom we believe is present with his whole being under the symbols of bread and wine, but we believe that we are joined with all other Christians, with every member of the human race, and with the whole of creation. Christ is in the hearts of all men and women and in the heart of all creation, sustaining everything in being. This mystery of oneness enables us to emerge from the Eucharist with a refined inward eye, and invites us to perceive the mystery of Christ everywhere and in everything. He who is hidden from our senses and intellect becomes more and more transparent to the eyes of faith — to the consciousness that is being transformed. The Spirit in us perceives the Spirit in others. (*HW,* 65)

Hebrews 1:3 NIV

The Son ... sustain[s] all things by his powerful word.

· *August 24* ·

All Creation Transformed

No longer I, but Christ lives in me....
Galatians 2:20 NAB

The Eucharist is the celebration of life, the dance of the divine in human form. We are part of that dance. Each of us is a continuation of Christ's incarnation, insofar as we are living Christ's life in our own lives — or rather, *instead of* our own lives. The Eucharist is the summary of all creation coming together in a single hymn of praise, surrender, and thanksgiving. In the Eucharist all creation is transformed into the body of Christ, transformed again into his divine person, and thrust into the depths of the Father for ever and ever. Even material creation has become divine in him. "For the creation," says Paul, "waits with eager longing for the revealing of the sons of God" (Rom. 8:19). (*HW,* 65)

Romans 8:19, 21 NRSV

For the creation waits with eager longing for the revealing of the children of God; ... creation itself will be set free from its bondage to decay and will obtain the freedom of the glory of the children of God.

· *August 25* ·

Just to Be

What we have to be is what we are.
Thomas Merton

Humility of heart is the capacity *just to be* for the sake of God. He called us into being. What more could one ask than the enjoyment of it? We did not ask for it; we did nothing to attain it. It *is;* and yet we cannot fully enjoy it without humility of heart. We always want to know, "What am I going to do with this being? Do I like it or don't I?" We are able to ask this question because we are free to be. And that freedom is what distinguishes us from the rest of material creation. One way of entering into this fundamental Christian attitude is to learn once again what it means *just to be* — to allow ourselves to rest before God with the being he gave us, with no other intention, effort, or purpose, except to surrender that being back to him. This is the orientation of contemplative prayer and the ultimate purpose of every genuine spiritual exercise. (*HW,* 68)

Psalm 91:1 NIV

He who dwells in the shelter of the Most High
will rest in the shadow of the Almighty.

· August 26 ·

Just to Do

Your joy will be complete.
Deuteronomy 16:15 NIV

Humility of heart is not only *just to be*. It is also the spontaneous capacity *just to do*. One cannot *just do* until he has first learned *just to be*. It is out of that experience of *just being* that one can then be content with the joy of *just doing*. *Just doing* does not mean that one does not have a purpose, does not think, does not plan. But in imposing one's will and intentions on reality and on events, one does not lose the basic experience and joy of *just doing*. As a child retains the joy of *just seeing* as it learns to distinguish between the various things that it sees, so we must be able to *do* without losing the capacity to judge. Our problem is that we get wrapped up in what we are doing and why we are doing it — analyzing it, planning, worrying about it — so that we lose the joy that is always available — *of just doing*. (*HW*, 68)

Deuteronomy 16:15 NIV

For the LORD your God will bless you in all your harvest and in all the work of your hands, and your joy will be complete.

· *August 27* ·

Two Great Gifts from God

LORD . . . We are the clay . . . You our potter. . . .
Isaiah 64:8 NASB

Just to be, just to do — these are the two great gifts of
God, the foundations of every other gift. We need to
return to these two great capacities again and again and
cultivate them. The events of daily life need to be placed
in perspective by a deep sense of prayer, by learning how
to *be* before God. Then, as reality comes in upon us,
we will perceive each event as the working of the Holy
Spirit, carefully designed for our particular needs. Every
event is a touch of the living finger of God, which is
sketching in us — body, soul, and spirit — the true image
of his Son, the being that the Father originally gave us
and which he is restoring. If we want to be anything
other than what God has made us to be, we are wasting
our time. It will not work. The greatest accomplishment
in life is to be what we are, which is God's idea of what
he wanted us to be when he brought us into being; and
no ideas of ours will ever change it. Accepting that gift
is accepting God's will for us, and in its acceptance lies
the path to growth and ultimate fulfillment. (*HW,* 69)

Isaiah 64:8 NASB

We are the clay, and You our potter;
And all of us are the work of Your hand.

· *August 28* ·

The Fullness of the Divine Plan

You will share in his divine nature.
2 Peter 1:4 NLT

The ascension is Christ's return to the heart of all creation, where he dwells now in his glorified humanity. The mystery of his presence is hidden throughout creation and in every part of it. At some moment of history, which prophecy calls the Last Day, our eyes will be opened, and we will see reality as it is, which we know now only by faith. That faith reveals that Christ, dwelling at the center of all creation and of each individual member of it, is transforming it and bringing it back, in union with himself, into the bosom of the Father. Thus, the eternal glory of the Trinity is achieved through the maximum sharing of the divine life with every creature according to its capacity. This is the fullness of the divine plan, "the mystery hidden for ages in God" (Eph. 3:9). (*HW,* 73)

2 Peter 1:4 NLT

He has promised . . . that you will share in his divine nature.

· *August 29* ·

The Grace of Pentecost

He who promised is faithful.
Hebrews 10:23 NIV

The Spirit of God, *the* promise of the Father, sums up in himself all the promises of Christ. For they all point to him. The incarnation is a promise. The passion and death of Jesus are promises. His resurrection and ascension are each a promise. Pentecost itself, the outpouring of the Spirit, is a promise. All are promises and pledges of the divine Spirit, present and to be received at every moment. He is the last, the greatest, and the completion of all God's promises, the living summary of them all. Faith in him is faith in the whole of revelation. Openness and surrender to his guidance is the continuation of God's revelation in us and through us. It is to be involved in the redemption of the world, in the divinization of the whole universe. To know that Christ is all in all and to know his Spirit, the ongoing promise of the Father — this is the grace of Pentecost. (*HW*, 75–76)

Hebrews 10:23 NIV

Let us hold unswervingly to the hope we profess, for he who promised is faithful.

· August 30 ·

May They All Be One

The Spirit of God dwells in you.
I Corinthians 3:16 NAB

Between God and us, two extremes meet: He who is everything, and we who are nothing at all. It is the Spirit who makes us one with God and in God, just as the Word is with God and is God — the Word by nature; we by participation and communication. Our Lord prayed for this unity at the Last Supper. Many of his words on that occasion find their fulfillment and ultimate significance in the outpouring of the Spirit into our minds and hearts.... Thus, we are not just *with* God in virtue of our baptism and our Christian vocation, we are *in* God. The Spirit is the gift of God, welling up in the Trinity from the common heart of the Father and the Son. He is the overflow of the divine life into the sacred humanity of Jesus, and then into the rest of us, his members. (*HW,* 76)

John 17:21 NJB

May they all be one, just as, Father, you are in me and I am in you, so that they also may be in us....

· *August 31* ·

Basic Thrust of Christian Spirituality

God replied, "I am who am."
Exodus 3:14 NAB

The basic thrust of Christian spirituality might be summed up in two texts from the Old Testament which speak to the fundamental situation of the human adventure. The first is from Exodus: "I am who am" (Exod. 3:14). God thus reveals himself as unlimited being. *Is-ness*. Everything that *is* must be in relationship to his infinite being, and in fact, penetrated by it. The other text is from Psalm 46:11: "Be still, and you shall know that I am God." We are thus invited to open ourselves completely to this infinite being, to the reality of the God who *is;* who penetrates, surrounds, and embraces us at every moment. God is the atmosphere that our spirit needs to breathe in order "to live, move, and have our being" (Acts 17:28). (*HW,* 80)

Psalm 46:10 KJV

Be still, and know that I am God....

· September 1 ·

Who Is God?

Who, O God, is like you?
Psalm 71:19 NIV

When you say *God*, you don't really mean *God*, you mean *your idea of God*. Or to put it another way, you mean *God as not God*. I say that because whatever we say about God is more unlike who God is than saying nothing. . . . All that words do . . . is to point in the direction of the mystery of the super-meaning of God. . . . We must be prepared to expand our idea of God. . . . It challenges our whole perception of reality. And let's face it, the reality that we see is for the birds. It doesn't exist. The way we see life is the tissue of our generic, educational, cultural, religious and whatever else conditioning. So we're often seeing what we want to see and nothing else. God has to fit into the little universe that we've built for ourselves growing up — which I call the *false self* — and which basically has *I* as the center of the universe. (*WG*)

Job 11:7 NIV

Can you fathom the mysteries of God?
Can you probe the limits of the Almighty?

· *September 2* ·

Beginning the Spiritual Journey

If you seek him, he will be found. . . .
1 Chronicles 28:9 NIV

As you know from the great work of Galileo, the earth, and still less *you*, is no longer the center of the universe. But seeing the universe from the *I* perspective is to see it inside out or upside down or not at all. This is a serious situation though it has existed this way since Adam and Eve. It's what might be called the *human predicament* or the *human condition*. It's the way *we* are, not the way *things* are or *reality* is. This shaking up of our idea of God, of Jesus Christ, of the Church, of the spiritual journey — the *shattering* of our ideas — is the true beginning of the real spiritual journey which is not about something but is a *way* — as Jesus said — the *way to nowhere*. And not many people want to go that way because it's a path into the unknown. But the unknown is where God actually is. (*WG*)

Deuteronomy 1:32 NIV

The LORD your God . . . went ahead of you on your journey . . . to show you the way you should go.

· *September 3* ·

Getting Acquainted with God

You still don't know me?
John 14:9 NRSV

To feel comfortable with this incredible... Presence is precisely the challenge that Jesus had when He introduced the Gospel. The first thing... [Jesus] seems to have done in His preaching career is to say, "Repent," a word that means not do penance in the sense of some external practice, but *change* the direction in which you're looking for happiness, implying that where we're looking for happiness is not the place where it is to be found and, still less, where God is to be found.... The contemplative dimension of the Gospel is precisely Christ's program for getting acquainted with the Ultimate Reality, as it really is, which is *no thing. No thing* in the sense of nothing particular. No concept. No experience. No feeling. It just is. Is. Is. Is. And the only way to find this *is-ness* is to *IS* too. And fortunately we have a good start because we all *are*.... The problem is who we think we *are*, is not the right gal or guy. We've got it... everybody else,... and... reality wrong. (*WG*)

John 14:9 NRSV

Have I been with you all this time...
and you still do not know me?

· *September 4* ·

Where Is God?

The kingdom of heaven is at hand.
Matthew 10:7 NAB

Let's look at Jesus' program for revolutionizing our idea of...God....All the ways that the people of his time were taught to think are systematically undermined and subverted one by one in the parables. For instance, the Pharisee and the publican. What Jesus is subverting is the idea that the *holy* is the place to find God. The last line must have shocked the hearers: the publican goes back to his home justified and the Pharisee goes back to his home unchanged because he's locked into his ethnological, social, civic and religious context....The hearers certainly said, "Is this man saying that the holy is not holy...that the...temple is no longer the place to find God...and that ordinary daily life is where the kingdom is to be found?"...The kingdom that Jesus is bringing...this revelation of where to find God and who he might be...is where? Right where you are! There's no place to go to find God and no place not to go....Everyday life is where God is most active and where holiness is to be found. (*WG*)

Luke 17:21 NIV

The kingdom of God is within you.

· *September 5* ·

Leaven, the Symbol of Corruption and the Unholy

The kingdom of heaven is like ... leaven. ...
Matthew 13:33 KJV

Another important parable that is earth-shaking in this revolutionary teaching of Jesus and which is crucial to understanding the contemplative dimension of the Gospel — that is making the Ultimate Reality accessible — is the parable of the leaven.... To grasp the depth of the meaning of the parable we have to know that leaven was the symbol of corruption to the Jewish hearer. It is the symbol of the unholy.... Jesus says an extraordinary thing: that the Kingdom of Heaven is in everyday life — everyday corruption.... The Kingdom of God in the Jewish mind had been compared to a great banquet.... or a cedar of Lebanon.... How can the symbol of corruption at the same time be the symbol of God's raising the poor and Israel and the oppressed to liberation — freedom — and ultimately domination of the world? (*WG*)

Matthew 13:33 KJV

The kingdom of heaven is like unto leaven, which a woman took, and hid in three measures of meal, till the whole was leavened.

· September 6 ·

Don't You Want to Meet Me as I Am?

Who is the LORD, that I should heed him. . . .
Exodus 5:2 NRSV

How can the God of Infinite Goodness have put up with Rwanda, Kosovo, the Holocaust? In other words *Who is God?* "Maybe I'm a fool to serve this God. . . . Why should I bother to pray?" These are big issues. . . . But at some point the God who truly is and was and is to come gets tired of being treated like an abstraction and says: "Don't you want to meet me as I am?" And since there's no chance of our changing without being challenged, God allows all kinds of misadventures and difficulties and usually hits us where it hurts the most. God has an uncanny capacity to put the divine finger on the thing that we most love, as if to say, "Would you kindly give me that?" To which our answer is, "Not a chance." . . . I think we need to be bounced around a bit by life before we can really get into this thing at a deep level. . . . The spiritual journey is a process and we're each at different levels of the process. That's why the question *Who is God?* is different for each of us. . . . *(WG)*

Numbers 33:12 KJV

And they took their journey out of the wilderness. . . .

· September 7 ·

The Doctrine of the Parables of Jesus Christ

My thoughts are not your thoughts....
Isaiah 55:8 NRSV

All I'm trying to communicate here is to question, as Jesus suggested in this parable of the leaven, that what you think is good may not be so hot and what you think is the most terrible evil that could happen to you, is perhaps the greatest experience you'll ever have of God in this life. This is the doctrine of the parables of Jesus Christ. And it's carried out in his own life. Who is this God who can say to His Son, "The hell with you!" — the Son of his bosom, the Son to whom he has communicated everything that the Father has in such a way that the Son is consubstantial. In other words, the life of the Son is not just a gift. It's all the Father is, expressed in the consubstantiality of the Son. (*WG*)

Isaiah 55:8–9 NRSV

For my thoughts are not your thoughts,
nor are your ways my ways, says the LORD.
For as the heavens are higher than the earth,
so are my ways higher than your ways
and my thoughts than your thoughts.

· *September 8* ·

God *Is* Love

> Beloved, . . . God is love.
> *1 John 4:7–8 NAB*

No one knows the Father like the Son because He emerged from the bosom of this Trinitarian Mystery that John says is love. Notice John doesn't just say God *shows* love. God *is* love. This is a huge distinction. The love of God *is* God. That means it's not sentimental. It's incredibly powerful. It's ruthlessly determined. It's determined to give itself away at any cost. And one problem we will have with the God who really is, is that he'll invite us to do the same. If it's not in this life, on your deathbed you finally have to say goodbye to the *false self.* You can't take it with you. (*WG*)

1 John 4:7–9 NAB

Beloved, let us love one another, because love is of God; everyone who loves is begotten by God and knows God. Whoever is without love does not know God, for God is love. In this way the love of God was revealed to us: God sent his only Son into the world so that we might have life through him.

· September 9 ·

God Joins Us in Our Suffering

For Thou art with me....
Psalm 23:4 THS

God doesn't take away our difficulties. He never said he would. He invites us to pray for anything we want. There's no guarantee of getting it. Because prayer is always answered but usually by God's giving us something better than we asked for only we don't recognize that yet.... God is not going to rescue you.... He joins you in your difficulties. This is a far greater gift than taking them away because it means that if you took them away you'd be where you were — just without those difficulties.... Suppose God joins you in your difficulties. Now you have a new attitude toward every difficulty and nothing can shake your peace of mind — even the greatest tragedies or sorrows. And little by little you begin to perceive that all suffering is in God and there's no other answer to explain it. (*WG*)

Psalm 23:4 THS

Yea, though I walk through the valley of the shadow of
    death,
I will fear no evil,
For Thou art with me;
Thy rod and Thy staff, they comfort me.

· September 10 ·

Redemption Means to Heal You from the Roots Up

[Jesus] healed those who needed healing.
Luke 9:11 NIV

Until . . . basic childhood programs for happiness are re-
pented of, that is to say *changed*, we're engaged, all of us,
in an addictive process which will show up if you live
long enough in a specific addiction unless you take the
spiritual journey to heart and a practice to heal that situation. The Gospel is about the healing of our conscious
and unconscious wounds. . . . It is into this melodrama of
everyday life that Jesus has come with the Kingdom and
that's where it works. That's where it's powerful. That's
where it's to be found on an everyday basis. Right where
you experience it and feel it. And it's the gift of Jesus.
And this is the full meaning of redemption — to heal you
from the roots up. So that instead of self-centered motivation and a world in which you see everything from
the perspective of the big *I am* of your ego, you see it
from the big *I AM* of God's selfless-self. . . . That is the
true view of reality. (*WG*)

Psalm 130:7 NIV

Put your hope in the LORD,
for with the LORD is unfailing love
and with him is full redemption.

· *September 11* ·

Basic Interconnection of All Creation

Holy Spirit, embrace all of us.

Nothing can hurt you if you can understand that whatever you are going through is your invitation to participate in the redemption of the world. That's why we say that Centering Prayer, as a movement into the spiritual journey, is a journey in which you take everyone with you — friends, enemies, relationships — and everybody benefits from your experience. And your prayer is not specified — at least during the time of Centering Prayer — but includes absolutely everyone, past, present and to come. Hence, not only are you re-doing the basic interconnectedness of everyone in the human species but also everything in all creation. So that everything belongs to you and you belong to everything. . . . It means that if anybody is suffering, you're suffering too with them. (*WG*)

Wisdom 12:1 *NJB*

[Lord,] your imperishable spirit is in everything!

· September 12 ·

Deep Knowledge of God

Christ is all and in all.
Colossians 3:11 NAB

In the Kingdom of Heaven Jesus says there is not Jew or Gentile, male or female, slave or free. But everyone is one in Christ. That's the way it actually is. We don't see it that way yet. That's the problem. What can we do to see it from right side up? It's the *deep* knowledge or the true knowledge of God that Paul presents to us in his epistles. Over and over again he speaks about *deep* knowledge. Not just knowledge. Not just intellectual knowledge. Not conceptual knowledge. But the kind of intimate knowledge that is only comparable to the most intimate kinds of human relationships. The deep knowledge of God — this is what he prays for his disciples. (*WG*)

Ephesians 1:7 NJB

May the God of our Lord Jesus Christ, the Father of glory, give you a spirit of wisdom and perception of what is revealed, to bring you to the full knowledge of him.

· September 13 ·

Where the Kingdom Is Most Active

Make sure my house is full....
Luke 14:23 NJB

The banquet is a symbol of the kingdom and those who show up at the banquet are the symbol of those who are actually saved. So this is an important parable about the kingdom.... The householder is the symbol of God the Father who has prepared this banquet of heaven.... "Go out into the highways and by ways...that my house may be filled."... The householder has to make a decision.... Either he cancels the banquet or he joins it. He joined it. This parable tells us from the One who knows God's heart or His bosom the best that this is the way God is. *Who is God?* For one thing, he joins everybody, and especially those nobody wants. So the neediest, the poorest, the most despised, the marginalized — here is where you can be sure the banquet is being served. Hence, the possibility of us joining these people if we want to be where the kingdom is most active. (*WG*)

Luke 14:23 NJB

Then the master said to his servant, "Go to the open roads and...press people to come in, to make sure my house is full...."

· September 14 ·

The Kingdom Is Christ Crucified

The cross . . . is the power of God.
1 Corinthians 1:18 NAB

We would like to escape from everyday life and our problems by a life of perfection or a life of virtue or a life of serenity like the Buddha manifests in his wonderful smile. Or we would like an apocalypse to rescue us from the oppressive situation we are in and give us a vindictive triumph over our enemies. This is the human response to difficulty. Jesus says, "Not a chance. No luck. That's not the kingdom." The kingdom, as Paul implies, is Christ crucified which is neither an escape to a world of virtue without difficulty or deliverance of a miraculous kind from our problems but in living with them with God and redeeming the world. That's the program of the parables. (*WG*)

1 Corinthians 1:23–24 NAB

Christ crucified . . . the power of God and the wisdom of God.

· *September 15* ·

Let God Introduce Himself

When you pray, go to your inner room....
Matthew 6:6 NAB

If you want to get to know who God is, why don't you let him introduce Himself? And here is how you do it. If you want to pray, Jesus says in Matthew 6:6, enter your inner room, close the door, and pray to your Father in secret and your Father who is in secret will reward you. Now this is the formula, if I understand it correctly, that is the umbrella diagram or map, you might say, of how to reach the deep knowledge of God — how to relate to the God who really is and not the God of our childhood imagination, projections, or ethnic or cultural limitations. (*WG*)

Matthew 6:6 NAB

But when you pray, go to your inner room, close the door, and pray to your Father in secret. And your Father who sees in secret will repay you.

· September 16 ·

Abba Is Not Like Any Father We Know

Awesome yet intimate is my God.

Not only does Jesus say the name of God out loud but he *changes* it. He uses a special term. *Abba* is the Aramaic which we translate as *Father*. But *Abba* is not like any father we know so if you had trouble with your own fathers — forget it, this is not a similar situation. God is Father in the sense of the absolute source of absolutely everything that is — the sustainer of all creation — the nurturer of our whole being at each of its levels from the most cellular to the full human development of the highest state of consciousness you can think of. So what Jesus is trying to emphasize with using the word *Abba* is that the Father that Jesus knows as God — the *Abba* — is close, is nurturing, is not only transcendent but also infinitely imminent, is not far away, is not just in heaven. There's no place to go to find Him. There's nothing to do to find Him. He's already here. (*WG*)

Galatians 4:6 NAB

As proof that you are [His] children, God sent the spirit of his Son into our hearts, crying out, "Abba, Father!"

· September 17 ·

Experience the God Who *Is*

Christ ... fills everything ... with his presence.
Ephesians 1:23 NLT

So even the words of Scripture that point to God are valuable in so far as they point but they cannot communicate the experience of the God who is, who was and is to come. It's only the presence of that God freely and totally presenting Himself to you. And what does that say? It says something about the heart of God we've got to know. And that is, He's not waiting for you to earn your keep, so to speak, or to impress Him with your virtues, or to do great works for God. He only is interested in *you* as *you*. You don't have to do a thing to win His love. Why? You've already got it! You don't have to do a thing to get into His presence. He's always there. This is the *right view of reality*. (*WG*)

Colossians 1:22 NLT

As a result [of Christ's death on the cross], he has brought you into the very presence of God, and you are holy and blameless as you stand before him without a single fault.

· *September 18* ·

We Believe God Is Present through Faith

Enlighten the eyes of your mind....
Ephesians 1:18 NJB

And so when we pray there's no question of God being present or absent. Our feelings may say, "I don't feel anything." So what? We're not our feelings. We decide to believe God is there because that's what our faith has revealed to us, and if you are doing a contemplative practice long enough you know this is true without anybody having to tell you because you have sensed and experienced some little touch of the presence of God. But it's a process, dear friends, and the taste that we have of God can continue to develop into ever deeper levels of intimacy that are absolutely inconceivable to us in the beginning — beyond anything, as Paul says, we could imagine or dream of is the closeness of God's presence. And it's a closeness that is totally loving, concerned, nourishing, supportive, sympathetic, empathic — every human relationship that is beautiful and good and true all rolled into one and multiplied millions of times over. (*WG*)

Ephesians 3:20 NJB

Glory be to him whose power, working in us,
can do infinitely more than we can ask or imagine....

· *September 19* ·

Divine Love

May you ... understand ... God's ... love. ...
Ephesians 3:18 NLT

What the Gospel is trying to tell us, especially in Christ's passion, death and resurrection, is that God is love in such a degree that at any cost — at *any* cost to God-self, He will give Himself to us. And that's the *deepest* meaning, it seems to me, of Christ's death and resurrection. It's God's signing on the dotted line that as far as God is concerned, His will to save everybody is so great that He'll go to any lengths, including the sacrifice of the Son of His bosom, in order to give us the maximum amount of divine life that we can possibly receive. So it reverses the whole misconception of a concept of God as a *just* God, the rewarder of the good, the punisher of the evil — which has a certain truth and has a certain basis for who God is — but is an inadequate, an immature way of understanding who God is. (*WG*)

Ephesians 3:18 NLT

And may you have the power to understand, as all God's people should, how wide, how long, how high, and how deep his love really is.

· *September 20* ·

The Heart of Christian Life

Be still and know that I am Love.
Nan C. Merrill

In contemplative prayer God has a chance to introduce Godself to you as merciful — infinitely merciful and tender.... That's why a practice leading to contemplative prayer [such as Centering Prayer] is so important. It's the *heart* of the Christian life. Without that, I venture to say, one does not understand what Christianity is all about. Its heart and soul is a contemplatively orientated relationship to God that partakes in Christ's own personal experience of the Ultimate Reality as *Abba* — that is Daddy, Papa, the Old Man. You cannot exaggerate the closeness, the gentleness, the tenderness of God but it is... not sentimental. It's a love that so wants to give us the treasure of the divine inner life — not just becoming better human beings. God's idea is to make us into Himself, that is, God by participation in the inner life of the Trinity which is totally giving, totally selfless. Unconditional love pouring itself out. And it has to pour itself out. That's the nature of infinite goodness. (*WG*)

Ephesians 2:4 NLT

God is so rich in mercy,
and he loved us so very much....

· *September 21* ·

Evil and the Heart of God

God sent his ... Son ... so ... we might have life....
1 John 4:9 NAB

There is no possibility of God holding back. It's from that perspective that you don't answer the question of evil but that you realize that without evil you would not get to understand the full extent of the heart of God which takes all suffering into itself and has, for love of us, sent into the world the Son of His bosom, the Beloved, to endure the utmost humiliation, death and rejection in order to convince us that God is willing, ready and *must* give Himself to us at any cost whatsoever. Somebody who has that insight is going to feel the need to do something similar. You can't receive that kind of love and be aware of it without realizing that it's a gilt-edged invitation to start doing the same. (*WG*)

1 John 4:9–11 NAB

God sent his only Son into the world so that we might have life through him. In this is love: not that we have loved God, but that he loved us and sent his Son as expiation for our sins. Beloved, if God so loved us, we also must love one another.

· *September 22* ·

Centering Prayer

Come to Christ, ... the living cornerstone....
1 Peter 2:4 NLT

So notice what Centering Prayer is — simply a point by point concretization of this advice of Jesus: "Enter your inner room." Where is that, please? It's obviously the spiritual level of our being. We move off our ordinary psychological everyday experience, the events, and people and our reactions to them and leave them outside. We enter our inner room ... a metaphor of the spiritual movement from the use of our ordinary everyday faculties in prayer to cultivating the spiritual level of our faculties — of our being — which are the intuitive intellect and the will toward God. (*WG*)

1 Peter 2:4–5 NLT

Come to Christ, who is the living cornerstone of God's temple. He was rejected by the people, but he is precious to God who chose him. And now God is building you, as living stones, into his spiritual temple.

· *September 23* ·

Knowledge of God through Jesus Christ

You will give me . . . joy in your presence.
Acts 2:28 NLT

And be prepared to move beyond . . . [the spiritual level
of our being] . . . to the true self which is deeper still and
finally enter into the inner sanctuary itself — God's presence within us — insofar as it is possible in this life —
which is the inmost center of our being and the direction
in which Centering Prayer is moving. . . . The reward
that is to be given is nothing less than the knowledge of
God through Jesus Christ. And why do we say through
Jesus Christ? Because we believe that Christ is truly the
Son of God and emerges eternally from the bosom of
the Father and is all that the Father is, that the Father
lives in the Son rather than in Himself. Thus, Jesus
could say, "He who sees me, sees the Father." Why?
Because there's nobody else there except the Father. In
other words, God has laid down God's life for us on the
cross. (*WG*)

John 14:6–7 NLT

I am the way, the truth, and the life. No one can come to
the Father except through me. If you had known who
I am, then you would have known who my Father is.
From now on you know him and have seen him!

· September 24 ·

Close the Door

I have stilled and quieted my soul....
Psalm 131:2 NIV

We...find ourselves in this inner room and find out
how much thinking goes on in our heads that we never
knew was going by and so lots of us can't stand it and
we get up and leave. If the "door is closed," at least you
may sit down again. Again, on a spiritual level, we might
interpret the "closed door" as closing the door on our
interior dialogue. That is to say, in many folks, there's
more noise in our heads — in our reflections — than
there is coming from outside. But all of this tumult and
noise needs to be left outside, according to Jesus' advice.
And so in Centering Prayer, we suggest closing the eyes
simply as a symbol of letting go of our environment to
join the people we're praying with at this deepest center
where we are bonded together and may experience and
gradually will experience our basic connectedness and
oneness. And there we pray to the Father in secret. Notice the cascading movement of secrecy to ever-deeper
levels of interior silence, with the reward of knowing
God as He really is at the end. (*WG*)

Psalm 131:2 NIV

I have stilled and quieted my soul;
like a weaned child with its mother,
like a weaned child is my soul within me.

· *September 25* ·

A Great Mystery

But then we will see face to face.
1 Corinthians 13:12 NRSV

This is a great mystery.... Anything we say about God
has a super-meaning and its real meaning is in relation to this inner experience that gradually alerts us and
sensitizes us to the presence of the *Abba* in everyone
else and — in fact — in all creation. Abba is so close to
us, closer than breathing, closer than living, closer than
dying. So close that you can't find Him because there
are no faculties that can recognize this mystery. It's so
direct that the only place we can experience its fullness
is in the light of glory where there are no more human
veils or limitations to shield us from the full force of the
divine light — life — the unconditional love. (*WG*)

1 Corinthians 13:8, 10, 12–13 NRSV

Love never ends.... When the complete comes, the partial will come to an end.... For now we see in a mirror,
dimly, but then we will see face to face. Now I know
only in part; then I will know fully, even as I have been
fully known. And now faith, hope, and love abide ... and
the greatest of these is love.

· September 26 ·

The Experience of the Inner Room

Quietly wait for the . . . LORD.
Lamentations 3:26 KJV

What goes on in the inner room? . . . The experience . . . begins with a commitment to Centering Prayer. . . . It begins with letting go of all our thoughts, our inner dialogue. The ultimate secrecy is no reflection on ourselves. That's the one that takes the most practice and discipline. It means that we don't judge the nature of our prayer. We don't say, for instance, this is better today than yesterday, or how great this peace feels or, if only I could stay here forever. All this is nonsense. Silence. Quiet. Stillness. Openness. Listening. These are all words that suggest themselves to someone who is beginning to taste the reality of God's presence within. But that taste is very far from the full meal. But as Paul says, we have to start out with milk because of our weakness. As time goes on, we get our teeth and our digestion gets able to consume the richer food of the Divine Presence. (*WG*)

Song of Solomon 5:1–2 KJV

I am come into my garden. . . . I sleep, but my heart waketh: it is the voice of my beloved that knocketh, saying, Open to me . . . my love. . . .

· *September 27* ·

Dealing with Childhood Problems

A new heart also will I give you. . . .
Ezekiel 36:26 THS

There is all the material in our conscious and unconscious . . . in which we developed false ideas of ourselves, false ideas of happiness, an idealized image of ourselves with which we are trying to compare ourselves to some standard. And all of these programs for happiness, based on the instinctual needs of security, power/control and affection/esteem, are simply the childish ways of dealing with the problems of early childhood. . . . Many of the traumatic experiences are repressed into the unconscious or prompt us to create programs to compensate or to hide from the pain of the frustration of emotional programs for happiness that are absolutely impossible to achieve or satisfy. For one reason, they have no limit. They're limit-less because a child has no faculties of moderation yet. (*WG*)

1 John 2:17 NRSV

And the world and its desire are passing away,
but those who do the will of God live forever.

· *September 28* ·

Office of the Divine Therapist

God ... will restore ... you.
1 Peter 5:10 NLT

So this inner room turns out to be the office of the Divine Therapist. And God, the greatest psychiatrist that ever was or will be, gradually leads us step by step. And by alternating consolation and desolation, reassurance and confrontation, with the truth about ourselves, this alternation gradually heals the wounds of a lifetime in a remarkable exercise of bringing us to self-knowledge that is not crushing or discouraging but rather illuminating and encouraging, because now we see that we're being gradually freed and healed from the very things that caused us the most physical and mental upset. (*WG*)

1 Peter 5:10–11 NLT

In his kindness God called you to his eternal glory by means of Jesus Christ. After you have suffered a little while, he will restore, support, and strengthen you, and he will place you on a firm foundation. All power is his forever and ever. Amen.

· *September 29* ·

All Things in God and God in All Things

I have chosen the way of truth....
Psalm 119:30 NIV

Thus, the Centering Prayer practice is a way of life, a commitment to a new life, to be a new creation, to become the true self which is God's idea of who we are; to let God act and bring us little by little to the integration of all reality into our understanding of God; and to see all things in God and God in all things. That is who God really is although we can never quite get our fingers or brains to hang onto him. You don't need to because God is much closer. The desire to feel God is a lack of faith because God, in fact, is already here. (*WG*)

Hebrews 10:22 NLT

Let us go right into the presence of God, with true hearts fully trusting him.

· *September 30* ·

Growing Awareness of God's Presence

The glory of . . . [God] filled the temple.
Ezekiel 43:5 NRSV

God is so secret, so close that you can't put your fingers on Him, because you're too close to Him. He is closer than anything you can imagine. And that is the insight that gradually emerges from allowing the Divine Therapy to accomplish its work and to bring you to a place where the feelings of absence or presence of God are totally irrelevant. More and more His ever-present awareness accompanies you like a fourth dimension to our three-dimensional world. Always loving. Always respecting your freedom. Always forgiving. Always present and becoming more and more present and developing us at every level into newer and more wonderful expressions of who this mystery, this reality beyond thinking might be like. (*WG*)

Ezekiel 43:4–5 NRSV

As the glory of the LORD entered the temple by the gate facing east, the spirit lifted me up, and brought me into the inner court; and the glory of the LORD filled the temple.

· *October 1* ·

Developing a Friendship with God

Have fellowship with God.
2 John 1:9 NLT

The spiritual journey has great difficulty in getting off to a good start if we are carrying a load of unexamined and unquestioned negative attitudes toward God. Our basic attitudes toward God are frequently solicited by circumstances and temptations to regress to former levels of relating that were childish and unworthy of God. We easily make judgments about God that are actually projections of our childish levels of consciousness. We also project on God the models of authority that we saw around us. If we had a dominating and authoritarian father, then God is easily felt to be dominating and authoritarian. If these influences were horrendous, then it becomes more difficult later in life to relate to God as God. Recognizing childish attitudes toward God and laying them aside will enable us to re-evaluate our relationship with God and to consider the possibility of making friends. (*IG*, 31)

Exodus 33:11 NASB

The LORD used to speak to Moses face to face, just as a man speaks to his friend.

· *October 2* ·

Source of Centering Prayer

You are ... the home of the living God. ...
2 Corinthians 6:16 TCLB

[The] ... source ... [of Centering Prayer] is the Trinity dwelling within us. It is rooted in God's life within us. ... With baptism comes the entire uncreated presence of the most holy Trinity: Father, Son, and Holy Spirit. We participate as human beings in God's life just by being alive, but much more through grace. We participate in the movement between the Father giving himself totally to the Son, and the Son giving himself totally to the Father. They empty themselves into each other. The Spirit of Love reconstitutes them, so to speak, so that they can keep surrendering forever. This stream of divine love that is constantly renewed in the life of the Trinity is infused into us through grace. We know this by our desire for God. That desire ... manifests itself in the effort that we make to develop a life of prayer and a life of action that is penetrated by prayer. (*IG*, 32)

2 Corinthians 6:16 NLT

For we are the temple of the living God. As God said: "I will live in them and walk among them. ..."

· October 3 ·

A Committed Relationship with Christ

The LORD delights in you....
Isaiah 62:4 NLT

As we sit in Centering Prayer, we are connecting with the divine life within us. The sacred word is a gesture of consent to the divine presence and action within. It is as if our spiritual will turned on the switch, and the current (the divine life) that is present in our organism, so to speak, goes on and the divine energy flows. It is already there waiting to be activated. Then as we sit in the presence of the Trinity within us, our prayer unfolds in relationship with Christ.... We go through a certain evolutionary process of acquaintanceship, friendliness, and friendship. The last implies a commitment to the relationship.... Friendship with Christ has reached commitment when we decide to establish a life of prayer and a program for daily life tailored to getting closer to Christ and deeper into the Trinitarian life of love. (*IG*, 33)

Jeremiah 29:12–13 NJB

When you call to me and come and pray to me, I shall listen to you. When you search for me, you will find me; when you search wholeheartedly for me, I shall let you find me....

· *October 4* ·

Centering Prayer

Oh, that we might know the LORD!
Hosea 6:3 NLT

Centering Prayer is focused on the heart of the Christian mystery, which is Christ's passion, death, and resurrection. Each time we consent to a new light on our weakness and powerlessness, we are in a deeper place with Christ.... Christ in his passion is the greatest teacher of who God is. Sheer humility. Total selflessness. Absolute service. Unconditional love. The essential meaning of the Incarnation is that this love is totally available. Centering Prayer is simply a humble method of trying to access that infinite goodness by letting go of ourselves. Consent to God's presence and action symbolized by the sacred word is nothing else than self-surrender and trust. (*IG,* 35)

Hosea 6:3 NLT

Oh, that we might know the LORD!
Let us press on to know him!
Then he will respond to us
as surely as the arrival of dawn
or the coming of rains in early spring.

· *October 5* ·

Redemption

> We wait for ... redemption. ...
> *Romans 8:23* NAB

The great privilege of contemplatives is that we are invited to share first in our own redemption by accepting
our personal alienation from God and its consequences
throughout our lives, and then to identify with the
divine compassion in healing the world through the
groanings of the Spirit within us. "The unspeakable
groanings of the Spirit," as Paul calls them, are our desires to bring the peace and knowledge of God's love
into the world. The love that is the source of those desires is in fact being projected into the world and is
secretly healing its wounds. We will not know the results of our participation in Christ's redemptive work in
this life. One thing is certain: by bonding with the crucified One we bond with everyone else, past, present,
and to come. (*IG*, 36)

Romans 8:26–27 NAB

The Spirit ... comes to the aid of our weakness; for we
do not know how to pray as we ought, but the Spirit
itself intercedes with inexpressible groanings. And the
one who searches hearts knows what is the intention
of the Spirit, because it intercedes for the holy ones
according to God's will.

· October 6 ·

Total Self-Surrender

Follow the way of love....
1 Corinthians 14:1 NIV

In human relationships, as mutual love deepens, there comes a time when the two friends convey their sentiments without words.... This loving relationship points to the kind of interior silence that is being developed in contemplative prayer.... The awareness of God's presence supplants the awareness of our own presence and the inveterate tendency to reflect on ourselves. The experience of God's presence frees us from making ourself or our relationship with God the center of the universe. The language of the mystics must not be taken literally when they speak of emptiness or the void. Jesus practiced emptiness in becoming a human being, emptying himself of his prerogatives and the natural consequences of his divine dignity. The void does not mean void in the sense of a vacuum, but void in the sense of attachment to our own activity. Our own reflections and acts of will are necessary preliminaries to getting acquainted with Christ, but have to be transcended if Christ is to share his most personal prayer to the Father, which is characterized by total self-surrender. (*IG*, 40–41)

Philippians 2:5 NLT

Your attitude should be the same that Christ Jesus had.

· *October* 7 ·

Opening to God's Presence Within

God...is with you wherever you go.
Joshua 1:9 NAB

Contemplative prayer, rightly understood, is the normal development of the grace of baptism and the regular practice of Lectio Divina. It is the opening of mind and heart — our whole being — to God beyond thoughts, words, and emotions. Moved by God's sustaining grace, we open our awareness to God, who we know by faith is within us, closer than breathing, closer than thinking, closer than choosing — closer than consciousness itself. Contemplative prayer is a process of interior transformation, a relationship initiated by God and leading, if we consent, to divine union. (*IG*, 41)

Deuteronomy 28:12 NAB

The LORD will open up for you his rich treasure....

· *October 8* ·

The Narrow Way That Leads to Life

He must increase; I must decrease.
John 3:30 NAB

Growth in divine union carries with it the need to di-
minish our human activity and to learn to wait upon
the Lord. It presupposes the gradual purification of
the sense faculties in the night of sense and the spiritual faculties in the night of spirit. Thus, the essence
of the contemplative path is not to be identified with
psychological experiences of God, though these may oc-
casionally occur. The essence of contemplation is the
trusting and loving faith by which God both elevates
the human person and purifies the conscious and unconscious obstacles in us that oppose the values of the
gospel and the work of the Spirit. Contemplative prayer
in the classic or strict sense of the term is "the narrow
way that leads to life." (*IG*, 45)

1 Timothy 1:14 NLT

Oh, how kind and gracious the Lord was!
He filled me completely with faith
and the love of Christ Jesus.

· *October 9* ·

Purification

Humble yourselves.... Purify your hearts....
James 4:7–8 NLT

At the allegorical level [of Scripture], we are now listening to the voice of Christ speaking through the readings we hear in the liturgy, savor in Lectio Divina, and recognize in the events of our own lives.... When you begin to experience this, you listen to the Scriptures in a very different way. They are not historical documents anymore, but stories about your own experience of the spiritual journey.... One other aspect of the allegorical sense of Scripture should not be passed over. This is the unloading of the unconscious, or purification. Purification occurs when, because of the trust and honesty that develops toward God as a result of a lively identification with the texts of Scripture, we are able to confront the darker side of our personality. We begin to experience the biblical desert. The biblical desert is not a place, but a state in which we experience inwardly what the passage of the Israelites through the desert and other similar texts symbolize outwardly. (*IG*, 49–50)

James 4:7–8 NLT

So humble yourselves before God.... Draw close to God, and God will draw close to you.... Purify your hearts....

· *October 10* ·

Trust God

Put your trust in the LORD.
Psalm 4:5 KJV

Contemplative prayer deepens the process of listening, and it does so by two experiences. One is the affirmation of our being at the deepest level, which comes through peace and spiritual consolation and enables us to entrust to God our whole story. Not that God doesn't know it already; he is just letting us in on the secret. Without trust in God, we cannot acknowledge the dark side of our personality, our mixed motivation, and our selfishness.... Deep prayer increases our trust in God so that we can acknowledge anything and are not blown away by it. Without that trust, we maintain our defense mechanisms. We try to hide from the full light of that realization. Like Adam and Eve, we hide in the woods. On the other hand, as our dark side is confronted, it is removed. By our acknowledging it, God takes it away. The process of contemplative prayer is a way of releasing what is in the unconscious. (*IG*, 51)

John 12:44 NLT

Jesus shouted to the crowds, "If you trust me, you are really trusting God who sent me...."

· *October 11* ·

Lectio Divina and Spiritual Growth

I am going to ... speak to her heart.
Hosea 2:16 NJB

According to the method of Lectio Divina, we just keep reading the Scriptures; that is all. We just keep listening, growing in trust, and growing in love as in any relationship. The Spirit who wrote the Scriptures is within us and enlightens us as to what the Scriptures are saying to us. The word is ultimately addressed to our inmost being. It starts with what is most outward and works toward what is most inward to awaken us to the abiding presence of God. When we are in the unitive understanding of Scripture, the outward word confirms what we already know and experience. (*IG*, 53)

Acts 16:14 NRSV

The Lord opened her heart to listen eagerly
to what was said by Paul.

· *October 12* ·

Silence

The LORD was . . . in the . . . silence.
1 Kings 19:12 NRSV

St. John of the Cross wrote, "The Father spoke one word from all eternity and he spoke it in silence, and it is in silence that we hear it." This suggests that silence is God's first language and that all other languages are poor translations. The discipline of Centering Prayer and the other traditional practices are ways of refining our receptive apparatus so that we can perceive the word of God communicating itself with ever greater simplicity to our spirit and to our inmost being. (*IG,* 55)

1 Kings 19:11–12 NRSV

"Go out and stand on the mountain before the LORD, for the LORD is about to pass by." Now there was a great wind, so strong that it was splitting mountains and breaking rocks in pieces before the LORD, but the LORD was not in the wind; and after the wind an earthquake, but the LORD was not in the earthquake; and after the earthquake a fire, but the LORD was not in the fire; and after the fire a sound of sheer silence.

· *October 13* ·

Strengthen Your Capacity for Interior Silence

I wait for the LORD, my soul waits....
Psalm 130:5 NRSV

The practice of Centering Prayer... might be called the first step on the ladder of contemplative prayer. As a rule we do not know when our prayer becomes contemplation in the strict sense. We only know that we are moving in this direction through our practice, and that the Spirit is moving toward us.... As our practice becomes more habitual, the action of the Spirit's gifts of wisdom and understanding become more powerful and gradually take over our prayer, enabling us to rest habitually in the presence of God. This experience is not necessarily felt during prayer, but is experienced in its effects in daily life. Waiting on God in the practice of Centering Prayer strengthens our capacity for interior silence and makes us sensitive to the delicate movements of the Spirit in daily life that lead to purification and holiness. (*IG*, 55)

Psalm 130:5–6 NRSV

I wait for the LORD, my soul waits,
and in his word I hope;
my soul waits for the LORD
more than those who watch for the morning,
more than those who watch for the morning.

· October 14 ·

Use of the Sacred Word

Raise your heart to God with ... love.
The Cloud of Unknowing

[During Centering Prayer] ... we use the sacred word
only as a focusing apparatus to bring our intention into
full clarity, whenever, because of the weakness of human
nature and the fact that the emotional programs for happiness in the unconscious are still active, we need some
means of returning to our original intention — that is,
consent to God's presence and action within us. With
regular practice, we develop a certain ease in promptly
letting go. We then enter into the cloud of unknowing,
which develops through repeated small acts of consent.
This means that we have dismantled the emotional programs sufficiently that we are alert to when they intrude
and can return to our original intention much more
promptly and, indeed, without necessarily returning to
the sacred word or sacred symbol. (*IG*, 64–65)

Revelation 3:20 NIV

Here I am! I stand at the door and knock. If anyone
hears my voice and opens the door, I will come in and
eat with him, and he with me.

· *October 15* ·

Centering Prayer

Love the Lord...with all your heart....
Mark 12:30 NRSV

The movement established by introducing the sacred word as the symbol of our intention to be open to God's presence and action brings us little by little to the spiritual level of our being, or, to use another analogy, to a general attentiveness to the river of consciousness itself rather than to what is passing along the surface of the river. The sacred word is simply the symbol of our intentionality. There is no special word, therefore, that is better than another, except that some words should be avoided because they spark an association of ideas and the tendency to think about other matters. In this prayer we are developing the capacity to wait upon God with loving attentiveness. The loving character is expressed by fidelity to the practice and patience while doing it. (*IG*, 65)

Mark 12:30 NRSV

You shall love the Lord your God with all your heart, and with all your soul, and with all your mind, and with all your strength.

· October 16 ·

Our Symbol of Intentionality

Speak, LORD, for your servant is listening.
1 Samuel 3:9 NRSV

The sacred word is a gesture of the consent of our spiritual will to God's presence in our inmost being. The word appears in our imagination but exercises no direct, quieting function on the level of our ordinary stream of consciousness. Rather, it only expresses our intention, the choice of our will to open and surrender to God's presence. This is the difference between Centering Prayer and a practice that utilizes some form of *attention*, as in looking at a candle, repeating a mantra, or visualizing some image. That is why we do not have to repeat the sacred word continuously. We only use it to maintain our intention of faith and love toward God. As long as thoughts go by like boats on the surface of the river without attracting our desire or causing an aversion, we do not need to return to the sacred word. In these instances, there is no interruption in the orientation of our *intention* toward God. (*IG*, 66–67)

1 Samuel 3:9 NRSV

If he calls you, you shall say,
"Speak, LORD, for your servant is listening."

· October 17 ·

The Gospel Program for Transformation

Let God transform you....
Romans 12:2 NLT

The gospel addresses the human condition just as it is. "Repent" — that fundamental call in the gospel to begin the healing process — means "change the direction in which you are looking for happiness." The various orientations for happiness that we brought with us from early childhood are not working. They are slowly killing us. If we respond to the invitation to repent addressed to us so lovingly by the divine physician, we can begin at once to take advantage of the Divine Therapy. Therapy ... implies both the relationship of friendship and the relationship of healing. Reading the gospel from the perspective of contemporary psychotherapy provides us with a detailed diagnosis of the disease. Contemplative prayer and action — life under the direct influence of the Seven Gifts of the Spirit (counsel, prudence, fortitude, reverence, wisdom, understanding, knowledge) — is the gospel program for human health, wholeness, and transformation. (*IG*, 74)

Romans 12:2 NLT

Let God transform you into a new person by changing the way you think. Then you will know what God wants you to do, and you will know how good and pleasing and perfect his will really is.

· *October 18* ·

The Kingdom of God

Seek ye first the kingdom of God....
Matthew 6:33 KJV

The [spiritual] journey, or process itself, is what Jesus called the Kingdom of God. This is a very important point. To accept our illness and whatever damage was done to us in life by people or circumstances is to partic- ipate in the cross of Christ and in our own redemption. In other words, the acceptance of our wounds is not only the beginning, but the journey itself. It does not matter if we do not finish it. If we are on the journey, we are in the Kingdom. This seems to be what Jesus is saying in the parables. It is in bearing our weakness with compas- sion, patience, and without expecting all our ills to go away that we function best in a Kingdom where the in- significant, the outcasts, and everyday life are the basic coordinates. The Kingdom is in our midst. (*IG*, 90–91)

Matthew 6:32–33 NLT

Your heavenly Father already knows all your needs, and he will give you all you need from day to day if you live for him and make the Kingdom of God your primary concern.

· *October 19* ·

Our Consent

Here I am, for you called me.
1 Samuel 3:8 NRSV

The divine energy is most powerful when it is least perceived by our faculties. When we sit down to do Centering Prayer and form our intention, we know the divine presence is already there. We do not create it. All we have to do is consent. The divine energy flows into us and through us. In its purest form it is available twenty-four hours a day at maximum strength. By consenting, we open to God as God is without trying to figure who or what God is. We consent to the divine presence without depending on a medium to express it, translate it, or interpret it in terms of our personal history, cultural conditioning, and temperamental bias. God communicates himself on only one condition. Our consent. (*IG*, 102–3)

1 Samuel 3:8 NRSV

The LORD called Samuel again, a third time. And he got up and went to Eli, and said, "Here I am, for you called me." Then Eli perceived that the LORD was calling the boy.

· October 20 ·

Spiritual Direction of Contemplatives

Your comfort gave me renewed hope....
Psalm 94:19 NLT

The method of Centering Prayer involves a good deal of interface with psychology; in fact, it was specifically developed as a dialogue between contemporary psychological models and the classic language of the Christian spiritual path. In the model of Centering Prayer, the heart of Christian purification lies in the struggle with unconscious motivations, and the prayer itself encourages the emergence of previously unconscious material. Thus, the spiritual director needs to be prepared for what emerges — not to assume the role of psychotherapist oneself, but to offer encouragement while recognizing when additional expertise may be called for. (*IG*, 107)

Psalm 94:19 NLT

When doubts filled my mind,
your comfort gave me renewed hope and cheer.

· *October 21* ·

Spiritual Direction According to Need

Instruct one another.
Romans 15:14 NIV

Spiritual direction should address itself to where each person is. Beginners on the journey need concrete instruction as regards the regular practice of prayer, a simple rule of life, and suggested readings. For those who are established in a prayer practice, there is need for Lectio Divina and study as well as practice for daily life. Several appropriate practices are suggested in the final chapter of my book *Invitation to Love*. ... In general, their goal is to encourage the contemplative attitudes of consent and a prompt letting go of afflictive emotions arising in daily life. And, of course, encouragement becomes essential as the dark night unfolds. (*IG*, 110–11)

Romans 15:14 NIV

I myself am convinced, my brothers [and sisters], that you yourselves are full of goodness, complete in knowledge and competent to instruct one another.

· October 22 ·

Support for Those More Advanced

[Speak] the truth in love. . . .
Ephesians 4:15 NASB

For those who are more advanced on the spiritual journey, the support of friendship and understanding is the
greatest gift one can offer. . . . The encouragement and
reassurance of one who has been over the same path and
the validation of one's own experience as coming from
God that only an experienced spiritual director can give
are enormous gifts. The best direction aims at enabling
or empowering the directee to graduate to the more refined and delicate guidance of the Spirit in all matters.
The director becomes a fellow traveler and friend on the
journey, and the directee and director speak the truth to
each other in love. Speaking just the truth can be too
harsh. Speaking the truth in love is mutually sustaining.
(*IG*, 111)

Romans 1:12 NLT

I'm eager to encourage you in your faith, but I also want
to be encouraged by yours. In this way, each of us will
be a blessing to the other.

· *October 23* ·

The Heart of the Spiritual Journey

Help me be present to God's Presence.

God has to lead us into a place that involves a complete reversal of our prepackaged values, a complete undoing of all our carefully laid plans, and a lot of letting go of our preconceived ideas.... This letting go into the unknown, this submitting to the unloading process, is an essential step into the mystery of our own unconscious. Hidden there is not only our whole life's history, especially the emotional wounds of early childhood buried in the warehouse of our bodies, but also the positive elements of our potential for growth in faith, hope, and divine love, and where the Divine Indwelling is also present. We must gradually recover the conviction, not just the feeling, of the Divine Indwelling, the realization that God — Father, Son, and Holy Spirit — is living in us. This is the heart of the spiritual journey, to which Centering Prayer is totally in service. (*IG*, 118–19)

Ephesians 3:16–17 NAB

That he may grant you in accord with the riches of his glory to be strengthened with power through his Spirit in the inner self, and that Christ may dwell in your hearts through faith....

· October 24 ·

Centering Prayer and Divine Love

Be filled with all the fullness of God.
Ephesians 3:19 NAB

[When we talk about Centering Prayer,] we are talking
...about love. This...distinguishes Centering Prayer
from Eastern methods [meditation]. Eastern methods
are primarily concerned with awareness. Centering
Prayer is concerned with divine love.... The Eastern
traditions put greater emphasis on what the self can do
and hence contain the innate hazard of identifying the
true self with God. The Christian tradition, on the other
hand, recognizes God present but distinct from the true
self. In other words, our uniqueness remains and becomes the vehicle for the divine expression, which was
why we were created: to share by grace in the oneness
of the Father and the Son. (*IG*, 125–26)

Ephesians 3:17–19 NAB

That you, rooted and grounded in love, may...know
the love of Christ that surpasses knowledge, so that you
may be filled with all the fullness of God.

· *October 25* ·

Centering Prayer, a Trinitarian Prayer

Grace...love...communion...be with you....
2 Corinthians 13:14 NKJV

Centering Prayer comes out of the Christian tradition and supports all the traditional devotions by illuminating their source. Thus it becomes the foundation for a much more fruitful apostolate and of relationships that are truly unselfish with other people, the cosmos, the earth, ourselves, and the Trinity. In other words, Centering Prayer is the Trinity living the divine life within us. It is eminently a Trinitarian prayer and implies the Incarnation, the Divine Indwelling, the Mystical Body of Christ, the Seven Gifts of the Spirit — the great dogmatic teachings that are generally regarded by theologians as the most important principles relating to the spiritual journey. (*IG*, 126)

2 Corinthians 13:14 NKJV

The grace of the Lord Jesus Christ, and the love of God, and the communion of the Holy Spirit be with you all.

· October 26 ·

Beyond Reflection and Vocal Prayer

He leads me beside the still waters.
Psalm 23:2 NKJV

There is an inherent movement from reflection to simply resting in God. Suppose you give a half hour to the rosary each day. Suppose as you are reflecting on the mysteries, you feel an inward attraction to be still in the presence of Our Lady and just absorb the sweetness of her presence with your inner spirit. You may sense the closeness of the divine presence within you as well as the closeness of Our Lady. This is what is meant by the term "resting in God." Moving beyond vocal prayers and beyond reflection when you feel the attraction to be still is the path to contemplation. This is the moment you should feel free to stop saying the vocal prayers and to follow the attraction to be still, because vocal prayers and discursive meditation are both designed to lead one gradually to that secret and sacred place. That is their whole purpose. (*IG*, 132)

Psalm 23:2 NKJV

He makes me to lie down in green pastures;
He leads me beside the still waters.

· *October 27* ·

Charismatics

"Peace, be still."...And there was a great calm.
Mark 4:39 KJV

To develop the contemplative dimension of the Gospel, charismatics have only to deepen their listening to the word of God in Scripture, remembering that this word also dwells within them. There is no opposition between the outward and inward word of God. They mutually confirm and reinforce each other. The inner word speaks in silence of intention, in the directness of love. The spoken word expressed in the proclamation of the Gospel or in the private reading of the sacred text is the same word that emerges from the eternal silence of the Father and is present in our inmost being where he awakens our understanding to the Divine mysteries to which his words point. It is not necessary to reject thinking, but only to go beyond it when attracted by the mysterious and absorbing presence of the Spirit. (*IG*, 146)

Psalm 16:9, 11 NIV

My heart is glad and my tongue rejoices;
my body also will rest secure....
You have made known to me the path of life;
you will fill me with joy in your presence....

· October 28 ·

Desire for God

I long for you, O God.
Psalm 42:1 NLT

We access [the Trinitarian life within] through faith, hope, and divine love. The exercise of these three theological virtues is precisely the transforming dynamism used by the Spirit to awaken in us the deeper levels of divine awareness. Paul says that "faith is the assurance of things hoped for" (Heb. 11:1). It is the invincible conviction that we are united to God before we can feel it or know it in any other way except through self-surrender. This is what opens the heart to what Paul calls the inpouring of divine love. "Hope does not disappoint us, because God's love has been poured into our hearts through the Holy Spirit that has been given to us" (Rom. 5:5). Thus the source of Centering Prayer, as a preparation for the contemplative life, is the Trinitarian life itself, which is going on inside us and is manifested by our desire for God, to seek the truth, and to pray. (*IG*, 151–52)

Psalm 42:1 NLT

As the deer pants for streams of water,
so I long for you, O God.

· *October 29* ·

The Focus of Centering Prayer

I want to know Christ. . . .
Philippians 3:10 NIV

The focus of Centering Prayer is . . . Jesus Christ. This
means that as we sit in faith, opening to the fullness of
the presence of God within us, we share the dynamic
of the Paschal mystery. In other words, when we stop
acting out of our false self and the emotional programs
for happiness by deliberately entering into silence and
solitude during the time of Centering Prayer, we are
immersing ourselves in a special way in the Paschal mystery. The Paschal mystery is Christ's passion, death, and
resurrection, the most comprehensive manifestation of
who God is, as far as this can be expressed in human
terms. . . . In the midst of a community praying together
in Centering Prayer is the Risen Christ. (*IG*, 152)

Philippians 3:10–11 NIV

I want to know Christ and the power of his resurrection
and the fellowship of sharing in his sufferings, becoming
like him in his death, and so, somehow, to attain to the
resurrection from the dead.

· *October 30* ·

Bonding with the Whole Human Family

With one heart... glorify... God....
Romans 15:6 NIV

Once we begin the spiritual journey, there is no longer
merely private prayer. Our prayer becomes a participation in the groanings of the Spirit for all the intentions
and needs of the human family. This does not mean that
we do not pray for our loved ones at other times. But it
does mean that during the periods of Centering Prayer
we enter into a sense of oneness with everyone else who
is experiencing grace, and with the whole human family. At times we may actually feel this bonding. This
bonding is the heart and soul of a Christian community.
(*IG*, 155)

Romans 15:5–6 NIV

May the God who gives endurance and encouragement
give you a spirit of unity among yourselves as you follow
Christ Jesus, so that with one heart and mouth you may
glorify the God and Father of our Lord Jesus Christ.

· *October 31* ·

Centering Prayer — Our True Self — The Mind of Christ

You have set my heart free.
Psalm 119:32 NIV

The presence of God is going to accompany us into daily life whether in other forms of prayer, in our relationships, or in our workplace. Without trying to, but just by being in God as you go about your daily functions, you exercise a kind of apostolate. In your very joking you may be pouring grace into the atmosphere and into other people. All our activities need to come out of this center. Centering Prayer tends not only to access our spiritual nature, but to express the true self. We are coming from an inner freedom that more and more, without our thinking about it, expresses the mind of Christ in our particular daily lives through the welling up and flowing over of the fruits of the Spirit and the Beatitudes. (*IG*, 159–60)

1 Corinthians 2:16 NIV

We have the mind of Christ.

· November 1 ·

Praying the Scriptures with Others

He opened their understanding....
Luke 24:45 NKJV

Praying the Scriptures in Common might be regarded as a kind of "Liturgy of Lectio Divina," or better, as a kind of shared "Liturgy of the Word." Praying the Scriptures in Common usually goes like this. A passage is read out loud three or four times followed by two or three minutes of silence. After each reading, the participants apply themselves inwardly to the text in specified ways. After the first reading, they become aware of a word or phrase. After the second reading, they reflect about the meaning or significance of the text. After the third reading, they respond in spontaneous prayer. After the fourth reading, they simply rest in God's presence, and after the period of silence, those who wish to do so are invited to share briefly on the text.... It is more appropriate to have such a "[Liturgy] of the Word" *after* a Centering Prayer period rather than before. Above all, the two practices should not be combined because each has its own integrity and uniqueness. (*AW*, viii, ix)

Matthew 18:20 NRSV

For where two or three are gathered in my name,
I am there among them.

· *November 2* ·

The Classical Practice of Lectio Divina

You show me the path of life.
Psalm 16:11 NRSV

The classical practice of Lectio Divina, however, can be divided into two forms: the monastic and the scholastic. The scholastic form divides the process following the reading of a passage of scripture four times into stages or steps in a hierarchical pattern: ... lectio [focus on a word or phrase], ... meditatio [reflect on the text], ... oratio [respond to the reflections], ... contemplatio [from time to time, move to a state of resting in God]. ... The scholastic method is a good way to learn Lectio Divina in the beginning, but at a certain point, when people have gotten the idea, it is time to try the monastic method because it is oriented from the start toward resting in God by establishing us in a listening attitude. (*AW*, viii, xii)

Psalm 16:11 NRSV

You show me the path of life.
In your presence there is fullness of joy;
in your right hand are pleasures forevermore.

· November 3 ·

The Monastic Way of Doing Lectio Divina

Dry bones, hear the word of the LORD!
Ezekiel 37:4 NIV

The monastic form of Lectio Divina is ... [an] ancient method and was practiced first by the Mothers and Fathers of the Desert and later in monasteries both East and West. It is oriented ... toward contemplative prayer. ... In the monastic way of doing Lectio Divina, we listen to how God is addressing us in a particular text of scripture. There are no stages, ladders, or steps in Lectio Divina; rather, there are four *moments* along the circumference of a circle. All the moments of the circle are joined to each other in a horizontal and interrelated pattern as well as to the center, which is the Spirit of God speaking to us through the text and in our hearts. To pay attention to any one of the four "moments" is to be in direct relationship to all the others. With this perspective, one may begin one's prayer at any "moment" along the circle and may move easily from one "moment" to another, according to the inspiration of the Spirit. (*AW,* viii–ix)

Ezekiel 37:4–5 NIV

Dry bones, hear the word of the LORD!
This is what the Sovereign LORD says to these bones:
I will make breath enter you, and you will come to life.

· *November 4* ·

Listen to Scripture

Listen to his voice today!
Psalm 95:7 NLT

The early monks read scripture aloud, so they were actually listening to it. They would then choose a phrase (or a sentence at the most) that impressed them. They would sit with that sentence or phrase without thinking of stages or following some predetermined schema, but just listening, repeating slowly the same short text over and over again. This receptive disposition enabled the Holy Spirit to expand their capacity to listen. As they listened, they might perceive a new depth to the text or an expanding meaning. A particular insight might also be singularly appropriate for them in their particular life situation or for the events of the coming day. According to scripture, the Spirit speaks to us every day. (*AW,* ix-x)

Psalm 95:7–8 NLT

Listen to his voice today!
The LORD says, "Don't harden your hearts...."

· *November 5* ·

Begin with Prayer to Holy Spirit

Spirit of the living God. . . .
2 Corinthians 3:3 KJV

This monastic way of doing Lectio Divina always begins with prayer to the Holy Spirit. The four moments along the circumference of the circle are: reading in the presence of God; reflecting, in the sense of ruminating (not in the sense of discursive meditation); responding with spontaneous prayer; and resting in God beyond thoughts and particular acts of the will. By "ruminating" I mean sitting with the text, allowing the Spirit to expand our listening capacity and to open us up to the deeper meaning of a text; in other words, to penetrate the spiritual sense of a scripture passage. This leads to the *faith experience* of the living Christ and increases the practical love for others that flows from that relationship. . . . We think the text but we do not think about the text. (*AW*, x–xi)

Romans 10:17 NLT

Faith comes from listening to this message of good news — the Good News about Christ.

· *November 6* ·

Grow in Union with the Eternal Word

Let the word of Christ dwell in you richly....
Colossians 3:16 NAB

In contemplative prayer, we are in touch with the source of all creation, hence, we transcend ourselves and our limited worldviews.... The fullness of the Godhead dwells bodily in Jesus, according to Paul. The Divinity begins to dwell in us bodily in proportion to our capacity to receive it as we grow in union with the Eternal Word. This process needs to be nourished both by the interior silence of contemplative prayer and by Lectio Divina (in the sense of listening). The awareness of the divine presence will also begin to overflow into ordinary activity. (*AW,* xii)

Proverbs 1:23 NLT

Come here and listen to me! I'll pour out the spirit of wisdom upon you and make you wise.

· *November 7* ·

Process of Conversion

Say "Yes" to Jesus.
Mother Teresa of Calcutta

The process of conversion begins with genuine openness to change....Grace is the presence and action of Christ in our lives inviting us to let go of where we are now and to be open to the new values that are born every time we penetrate to a new understanding of the Gospel. Moreover, Jesus calls us to repent not just once; it is an invitation that keeps recurring. In the liturgy it recurs several times a year, especially during Advent and Lent. It may also come at other times through circumstances: disappointments, personal tragedy, or the bursting into consciousness of some compulsion or secret motive that we were not aware of. A crisis in our lives is not a reason to run away; it is the voice of Christ inviting us to accept more of the divine light. More of the divine light means more of what the divine light reveals, which is divine life. And the more divine life we receive, the more we perceive that divine life is pure love. (*AW,* 4–5)

Acts 26:18 KJV

Open their eyes, and...turn them from darkness to light....

· *November 8* ·

Each Time We Consent
to an Enhancement of Faith

And their eyes were opened.
Matthew 9:30 NRSV

Each time we consent to an enhancement of faith, our
world changes and all our relationships have to be ad-
justed to the new perspective that has been given to us.
Our relationship to ourselves, to Jesus Christ, to our
neighbor, to the Church — even to God himself — all
change. It is the end of the world we have previously
known and lived in. Sometimes the Spirit deliberately
shatters those worlds. If we have depended upon them
to go to God, it may feel as if we have lost God. We
may have doubts about God's very existence. It is not
the God of faith we are doubting, but only the God of
our limited concepts or dependencies; this god never existed anyway. Pure faith is the purification of the human
props in our relationship to God. (*AW,* 5)

Matthew 9:28–30 NRSV

Blind men came to him; ... [Jesus] touched their eyes
and said, "According to your faith let it be done to you."
And their eyes were opened.

· *November 9* ·

Repent and be Willing to Change

I have come to do your will, O God.
Hebrews 10:7 NIV

If you repent and are willing to change, or willing to let God change you, the kingdom of God is close. In fact, you have it; it is within you and you can begin to enjoy it. The kingdom of God belongs to those who have let go of their possessive attitude toward everything including God. God is pure gift; we cannot possess him just for ourselves. We can possess him only by receiving him and sharing him with others. (*AW,* 5–6)

Philippians 2:13 NIV

It is God who works in you to will and to act according to his good purpose.

· November 10 ·

Follow the Inspiration of the Spirit

All things are possible with God.
Mark 10:27 NIV

In daily life the Spirit is speaking in various ways. Christ is present under different disguises. In human tragedy, there is something that the Father wants us to do to bring healing. The contemplative dimension of the Gospel keeps heightening this sensitivity. When one follows the inspiration of the Spirit, results occur that could not possibly have been foreseen. Hence, the need to cultivate God's presence and action in situations that seem impossible to do anything about. The mystery of Christ is at work in everything, however humble or humdrum. Our response can be inspired by the false self or by the Spirit. If it is by the Spirit, the consequences are immense ... for ourselves, for others, and perhaps for the whole human family. (*AW,* 10–11)

Mark 10:27 NIV

Jesus ... said, "With man this is impossible, but not with God; all things are possible with God."

· *November 11* ·

Listen to Matthew 14:29–31 in the Spirit of Lectio Divina

In whirlwind and storm is His way....
Nahum 1:3 NASB

Little by little we are able to hear the still small voice in the hurricane, the earthquake, or the fire. God is hidden in difficulties. If we can find him there, we will never lose him. Without difficulties, we do not know the power of God's mercy and the incredible destiny he has for each of us. We must be patient with our failures. There is always another opportunity unless we go ashore and stay there. A No-risk situation is the biggest danger there is. To encounter the winds and the waves is not a sign of defeat. It is a training in the art of living, which is the art of yielding to God's action and believing in his love no matter what happens. (*AW,* 15)

Matthew 14:29–31 NLT

Peter . . . walked on the water toward Jesus. But when he looked around at the high waves, he was terrified and began to sink. "Save me, Lord!" he shouted. Instantly Jesus reached out his hand and grabbed him. "You don't have much faith," Jesus said. "Why did you doubt me?"

· *November 12* ·

Listen to the Word of God from Matthew 15:21–28

O woman, great is your faith!
Matthew 15:28 NAB

How do we find God in his apparent absence, rejection, and abuse? . . . [The] . . . episode [of the Canaanite woman] is a description of how to respond when prayer gets difficult, when the interior life falls to pieces. . . . "It is not right," Jesus says, "to take the food of the children and to throw it to dogs." How could Jesus say such a thing? The Canaanite woman is not put off by this insult any more than she was by his silence and rejection. She answers in effect, "Lord, you are right. But have you thought of this possibility? I'm not asking for the food of the children; I'm not asking for a loaf of bread. Even the dogs under the table sometimes pick up a few crumbs that fall by mistake. How about dropping me one of those crumbs?" Jesus responds, "Oh my dear lady, your faith is terrific! . . . " Everything belongs to those who have reached this level of faith. (*AW,* 17, 19)

Matthew 15:28 NAB

Then Jesus said to her in reply, "O woman, great is your faith! Let it be done for you as you wish." And her daughter was healed from that hour.

· *November 13* ·
_____

Listen to the Word of God
from John 8:1–11

Jesus said, . . . "Go and sin no more."
John 8:11 NLT

In this story we see Jesus offering his great mercy to
the sinful woman, but notice that the words with which
he rescued her are an invitation to the accusers to enter
into their own consciences and to see what is wrong
with them. . . . When Jesus said, "Let the man without
sin throw the first stone," He is saying to the accusers,
"How about looking into your own consciences?" . . .
The accusers of the woman thought they were uphold-
ing the Law; they did not recognize their hypocrisy in
using the Law in order to entrap Jesus. He invited them
to look into their consciences and face the pride that was
motivating their malice. The basic question is always:
What is your motive for this act? It is an invitation to
conversion, to take full responsibility for ourselves, our
community, nation, and religion. (*AW*, 23–24)

John 8:7 NLT

Let those who have never sinned throw the first stones!

· *November 14* ·

Accessing the Eternal Dimension within Us

Sacrament of the present moment!
Jean-Pierre de Caussade

The Second Coming of Christ can occur in two ways:
with the end of time (only God knows when that is)
or by our accessing the eternal dimension within us.
The latter is what the liturgy and the spiritual journey
are attempting to bring about. The values of eternal
life are constantly breaking into the linear dimension of
chronological time and putting us in contact with the
Ultimate Reality.... In each moment of chronological
time, the divine value of each moment is available to us
in proportion to our sensitivity to the Spirit of Christ.
The Spirit suggests what is to be done at each moment
in our relationship to God, ourselves, other people, and
the cosmos. (*AW,* 35–36)

Revelation 2:7 NLT

Anyone who is willing to hear should listen to the Spirit
and understand what the Spirit is saying....

· November 15 ·

Cure of the Blind Man
in the Spirit of Lectio Divina

Lord, help me to see with eyes of faith.

The awakening of the spiritual senses is the call of the gospel to see with the eyes of faith. When the spiritual senses are activated, then we truly hear, then we truly see; we have the receptive apparatus to open to the heart of reality. Through faith, hope, and charity we hear the ultimate message of the universe. The result of that awakening is symbolized in what the blind man did on receiving his sight: he followed him. Jesus emphasizes what healed him. Faith! This was not just the faith that works through reason, but the faith that is a direct intuition. "Go in peace," he says to this man, "your faith has saved you." Your faith, that is, your consent to God calling you, touching you, transforming you. Transformation in Christ is the ultimate healing. (*AW*, 39–40)

Mark 10:51–52 NAB

[Jesus asked,] "What do you want me to do for you?" The blind man replied to him, "Master, I want to see." Jesus told him, "Go your way; your faith has saved you." Immediately he received his sight and followed him on the way.

· *November 16* ·

The Penitent Woman
in the Spirit of Lectio Divina

Your faith has saved you; go in peace.
Luke 7:50 NAB

Actually, personal sin is not the problem. . . . It is the false self with its orientation to prefer ourselves to others, including God. Out of that diseased root comes all the rotten fruit that the false self produces. Whether a bad tree produces a lot of apples or only a few, all the fruit is inedible. So we have to entrust the whole tree, root and branches, to the mercy of God who alone can heal the radical distortion of the human condition. This is what conversion is. It is not a Band-Aid approach to life. It is the radical letting go of our programs for self-centered happiness in the form of personal or collective security, power and control over others, and unlimited pleasure, affection and esteem. That is the sickness. . . . To heal the disease requires a conversion as deep as that manifested by the penitent woman. . . . Faith means trust in the infinite mercy of God manifested in the redemptive work of Jesus. This is what saved the penitent woman; it can save each of us. (*AW*, 53)

Luke 7:50 NAB

[Jesus] . . . said to the woman, "Your faith has saved you; go in peace."

· *November 17* ·

Love One Another *as Jesus Loved Us*

Carry Jesus wherever you go.
Mother Teresa of Calcutta

[Jesus said to the scribe], "You are not far from the king-dom of God." In other words, the kingdom of God requires something more than [to love God and] to love our neighbor as ourselves. To love our neighbor from the perspective of the true self, as one possess-ing the image of God, is a great insight, but it still is not the fullness of the kingdom of God according to Jesus. A new commandment characterizes the Christian faith which carries the insight of the scribe a step fur-ther. It is to love one another *as Jesus has loved us.* This is much more difficult. This is to love others in their individuality...and in the things that drive us up the wall, to love our neighbor, in other words, just as they are with each one's... unbearable habits, unreasonable demands, and impossible characteristics. The new com-mandment is to accept others unconditionally; that is to say, without the least wish to change them. To love them in their individuality is the way Jesus has loved us. (*AW,* 56)

Mark 12:34 NRSV

When Jesus saw that he answered wisely, he said to him, "You are not far from the kingdom of God."

· November 18 ·

Our Lady of Sorrows

[Jesus said,] "She is your mother."
John 19:27 NLT

Mary is the paradigm of those who are manifesting Christ in their individual lives. Her compassion was rooted in the kind of love that God has for us — a love that is tender, firm, and completely self-giving. God-consciousness is the fruit of Christ's passion, death, resurrection, and ascension. In the ascension Jesus enters with his humanity into the heart of all creation where he dwells everywhere and in everything, visible only to the X-ray eyes of faith that penetrate through every disguise including the greatest of sorrows. God is reigning despite all appearances to the contrary. The risen Christ is ever-present, opening the way for the final triumph of God in which, as Paul says, "God will be all in all." This is the faith that Mary had when she looked on what was left of the flesh of her son and yet saw him reigning from the cross — the triumph of God hidden in the greatest suffering. This makes her our companion and support in every conceivable trial. (*AW,* 60)

Revelation 19:6 NLT

For the Lord our God, the Almighty, reigns.

· November 19 ·

Divine Compassion

Jesus, remember me....
Luke 23:42 NAB

John's Gospel perceives Jesus reigning from the cross.
Divine love is triumphing over the apparent victory of
worldliness, violence, and sin. Anyone who accepts that
vision is reigning with Christ in the kingdom right now.
To paraphrase Jesus' words to the good thief, "You are in
paradise right now even amidst your sufferings." Thus,
as soon as we open ourselves to divine love, our sins
are forgiven and forgotten. We are instantly placed, like
the good thief, in the reign of divine love. Thus, as the
value systems of this world are reversed and selfishness
is crucified in the body of Christ, divine love is poured
out over the human family and made available to everyone who consents. The reign of Christ the King is not
a reign of power but of compassion. He invites us to
participate. (*AW,* 62)

Luke 23:42–43 NAB

Then he said, "Jesus, remember me when you come into
your kingdom." He replied to him, "Amen, I say to you,
today you will be with me in Paradise."

· *November 20* ·

Reflect on God's Loving Presence

You must be ready all the time....
Luke 12:40 NLT

[In the parable about the head of the house staying awake if he knew when the thief was coming], Jesus represents himself as an unexpected intruder. This parable refers not just to physical death, but to all his unexpected intrusions into our lives that take us by surprise. Sometimes he comes when we are at our lowest ebb. All of a sudden, in the midst of anguish, anger, bitterness, lustful thoughts, and the feeling of abandonment, this incredibly loving presence appears as if to say, "Well, what is the matter with you? What are you belly-aching about? Because it got a little dark, you didn't see me. Be on guard, therefore, because the son of man will come when you least expect him." When we least expect him is the darkest part of the night. It is not our pleas that bring the master back; he comes when he sees that we have completed our preparation. The pain of waiting is in proportion to the joy of resurrection. To those on the spiritual journey nothing happens that is not directed toward divine union if they only say "Yes." (*AW,* 70–71)

Luke 12:40 NLT

The Son of Man will come when least expected.

· November 21 ·

Imitate God's Compassion toward Us

Love is a fruit always in season.
Mother Teresa of Calcutta

Love alone can change people. This is the great confrontation that no one can resist. It offers others space in which to change no matter what they do. Our ill-conceived efforts, especially if they arise from personal annoyance or because the conduct of others might cause us embarrassment, will accomplish nothing. The offenders will sense that the confrontation is not coming from a genuine concern for them and will mobilize their defenses. By showing love no matter what happens we provide them with a milieu in which they can experience the possibility of changing. This is to imitate God's compassion toward us. He is constantly trying to correct us but never with vindictiveness.... He simply keeps inviting us to let go of conduct that is self-destructive and to come back to his love. Whenever there is something to be corrected, he indicates that if we amend, we will enjoy complete forgiveness. The only confrontation that leads to correction is to accept whomever we are trying to help just as they are. (*AW,* 78)

Jeremiah 31:3 NLT

Long ago the LORD said... "I have loved you, my people, with an everlasting love. With unfailing love I have drawn you to myself...."

· *November 22* ·

Open to the Values of the Gospel

Lord, help me live the values of Christ.

[Jesus]...presented...[the crowd] with the wisdom saying...which I paraphrase:..."Unless you are ready to turn your backs on the people who are closest to you, you cannot be my follower." Then he added, "You also have to hate your own life, your very self, your own thoughts, judgments....Don't just follow me blindly...." The sayings of Jesus are designed to move people to question their unquestioned values so that they can be open to the radical program for change that he offers....When we are called, as Jesus is implying, to a higher set of values that involves the service not just of our immediate family...then these unquestioned values stand in the way. Hence, Jesus warns, if the accepted values oppose or prevent us from growing beyond them, we must "hate" our cultural attachments and launch out into the unknown. We must be ready to renounce the values we have interiorized when these oppose the values of the Gospel. (*AW,* 82–83)

Luke 14:33 NJB

None of you can be my disciple without giving up all that he owns.

· *November 23* ·

Enter through the Narrow Door

The door to heaven is narrow.
Luke 13:24 NLT

In the course of . . . [Jesus'] teaching, someone asks, "Sir, are there going to be few or many saved?" . . . Jesus replies, "Try to enter through the narrow gate." What is the narrow door that provides such great security? In a sheepfold the gate is extremely narrow. Only one sheep can go in or out at a time. Hence, there is an intimate relationship between the shepherd and the sheep. He calls each one by name. The narrow door, in the context of Jesus' journey to Jerusalem and to his sacrificial death, is his teaching and example. It is not calling oneself a Christian but actually following Jesus that counts. The basic teaching of Jesus is the unconditional acceptance of everyone. Although such a practice is extremely demanding, everyone has the capacity to do it because only two things are required — suffering and love. Everyone can suffer and everyone can love. (*AW,* 86–87)

Luke 13:23–24 NLT

Someone asked him, "Lord, will only a few be saved?" He replied, "The door to heaven is narrow. Work hard to get in. . . . "

· *November 24* ·

Reflect on New Wine in Fresh Skins

Put new wine in fresh skins....
Matthew 9:17 NJB

New wine is a marvelous image of the Holy Spirit. As we move to the intuitive level of consciousness through contemplative prayer, the energy of the Spirit cannot be contained in the old structures. They are not flexible enough.... The new wine is the contemplative dimension of the Gospel. Its basic act is consent to the presence and action of the Spirit within us. This consent is directed not to our intentionality but to God's intentionality. The Spirit who loved us first is pouring the wine, not we.... If we consent to God's intentionality, he works in us through the fruits of the Spirit: boundless compassion, joy, peace, and the others enumerated by Paul (Gal. 5:22–23). (*AW,* 89–91)

Galatians 5:18 NJB

You are led by the Spirit....

· *November 25* ·

The Material Universe Becomes Divine

The glory of the Lord shone round them.
Luke 2:9 NJB

Events and images in Scripture symbolize inner experiences. Christmas is, therefore, an important occasion in our personal history. Through it God awakens us to the divine life in us. We are not only human beings; we are divinely human beings. The angels, by word and action, impressed upon the shepherds the meaning of the newborn child. The liturgy tries to do the same by word and sacrament.... Now God has become one of us and is breathing our air. In Jesus, God's heart is beating; his eyes are seeing; his hands are touching; his ears are hearing. Through his humanity, the whole material universe has become divine.... By becoming a human being, he is in the heart of all creation and in every part of it. (*AW*, 95–97)

Matthew 1:23 NLT

Look! The virgin will conceive a child! She will give birth to a son, and he will be called Immanuel (meaning, God is with us).

· *November 26* ·

Practical Advice from Mary

"Do whatever he tells you."
John 2:5 NIV

Our Lady is the heart of the human response to God because her consent is the source of everyone's consent. We will never consent to God as fully as we can until we understand what her consent really meant. She gave the most practical advice of all time in her offhand remark to the waiters at the marriage feast of Cana. "Do," she said, "whatever he tells you." That is precisely what she did. To do the will of another is, in a sense, to become the other. To do God's will is to lose one's own separate identity. To consent to the fact of God's interior presence is to know where you came from and where you are going. It is to know who you are. "Do you consent to become divine?" That is the question asked of us today. The second question is more concrete. "Will you consent to express me, your God, in your body?" That is scary! To be God in everything we say and do and are! Such is the radical consent that our Lady gave. (*AW,* 99–100)

John 2:5 NIV

His mother said to the servants,
"Do whatever he tells you."

· *November 27* ·

Mysterious Inward Death and Rebirth

God, help me to see with Your eyes.

Joseph became the husband of Mary only after he had given up his plan to marry her. . . . The loss and finding of Mary . . . parallels the loss and finding of Jesus in the Temple, . . . an even deeper participation in the mystery of Christ's passion, death and resurrection. Every true seeker of God, from the beginning of time to the end of the world, has to pass through this mysterious inward death and rebirth, perhaps many times over. Joseph's love of Mary and his vision of life with her — and later his love of Jesus and his vision of life with him — were his two great visions, both given to him by God and both seemingly taken away from him by circumstances God arranged. These were the two eyes that he had to give up in order to see with God's eyes. He had to surrender his personal vision in order to become *Vision itself.* That . . . is the goal . . . of Christian life. (*AW,* 101–2)

Luke 2:46, 48–50 NLT

Three days later they finally discovered him. He was in the Temple. . . . His parents didn't know what to think. . . . "[We] have been frantic, searching for you everywhere." . . . [Jesus said,] "You should have known that I would be in my Father's house." But they didn't understand what he meant.

· *November 28* ·

Divine Hospitality

I have set you an example....
John 13:15 NIV

Jesus washed the feet of his disciples. They were to be his guests at the first eucharistic supper, just as we are his guests at the commemoration of it. This sharing in the body and blood of the god-Man is the pledge of a still greater banquet: the eating and drinking of immortal life and love at the eternal banquet of heaven, where our nourishment will be the divine essence itself.... How can we thank the Lord for his invitation, for the incredible depth of his sharing? Having purified our hearts by stirring up the grace of our baptism and looking forward to the fullness of the Spirit that we hope to receive, we consume the flesh of Christ which, like a live coal, bears within itself the eternal flame of the Spirit. As we receive Jesus into our hearts, our inmost being is set afire, and we are turned in the direction of the deepest reality of human life, the presence of the Trinity in the depths of our spirit. (*AW,* 108–10)

John 13:1 NLT

[Jesus] showed the disciples the full extent of his love.

· *November 29* ·

Love with Divine Love

Love each other as I have loved you.
John 15:12 NIV

To love as Jesus loved us is to love with Divine Love, with the Love of the persons of the Trinity, which is total self-surrender. They love not in order to receive love in return, but because it is the nature of divine love to give, to pour itself out, to surrender, and to do so for no other reason than because it is what it is — sheer gift. We too must love not in order to become something, but because we are called to be stewards of divine love; to be identified with it and to be channels for this immense energy, till the world is transformed by Christ and he is all in all. We surrender not because we choose to, but because Jesus has chosen us and commanded us to love as he has loved us. (*AW*, 117–18)

John 15:12, 16 NIV

My commandment is this: Love each other as I have loved you.... You did not choose me, but I chose you and appointed you to go and bear fruit — fruit that will last.

· November 30 ·

Humility

My soul magnifies the Lord....
Luke 1:46 NRSV

The eternal Word emerges from the Father without any separation. He steps forth into the world without ever leaving the Father. He works in this world, while remaining at perfect rest in the bosom of the Father. He acts, but always abides in his source. Jesus, the Word made flesh, recommends that we too act without ever losing the awareness of our Source. "As the living Father sent me, and I live because of the Father, so he who eats me will live because of me" (John 6:57). As Jesus is united to the Father as his Source, so we are to be united to Jesus as our Source. How? Through the same means that our Lady exercised and now shares with us through the grace of her Assumption — the acceptance of our insignificance. (*AW*, 120–21)

Luke 1:46–48 NRSV

Mary said, "My soul magnifies the Lord, and my spirit rejoices in God my Savior, for he has looked with favor on the lowliness of his servant...."

· December 1 ·

The Liturgical Year

Share in the glory of our Lord....
2 Thessalonians 2:14 NIV

The Liturgical Year focuses on the three great theological ideas that form the heart of Christian revelation: divine light, life and love. They constitute the gradual unfolding of what we mean by grace, God's gratuitous sharing of his nature with us. As the primary focus of divine activity, each emphasizes a special stage or aspect of God's self-communication. These theological ideas are all contained in condensed form in each celebration of the Eucharist. In the Liturgical Year they are expanded in order to be studied and savored one by one, the better to search out and assimilate the divine riches contained in each of them. (*MC*, 4)

2 Thessalonians 2:14 NIV

[God]...called you to...our Gospel, that you might share in the glory of our Lord Jesus Christ.

· *December 2* ·

Humanity Invited into the Divine Relationship

Humbly welcome the Word....
James 1:21 NJB

The prologue of John introduces us to the eternal plan of God in which Christ has the central position. The Eternal Word, the silence of the Father coming to full expression, has entered the world and manifested as a human being. Because of his infinite power, the Eternal Word has taken the entire human family into his divine relationship with the Father. We who are incomplete, confused and riddled with the consequences of original sin constitute the human family that the Son of God took upon himself. The basic thrust of Jesus' message is to invite us into divine union, which is the sole remedy for the human predicament. (*MC*, 5)

John 1:12–13 NLT

To all who believed him and accepted him, he gave the right to become children of God. They are reborn! This is not a physical birth resulting from human passion or plan — this rebirth comes from God.

· December 3 ·

The Gospel Addresses
Our Search for Happiness

Repent and believe in the gospel....
Mark 1:15 NASB

Lacking the experience of divine union, we feel alienated from ourselves, God, other people and the cosmos.
Hence, we seek substitutes for the happiness for which
we are predestined but which we do not know how to
find. This misguided search for happiness is the human
predicament that the Gospel addresses. The first word
that Jesus speaks as he enters upon his ministry is "repent," which means, "change the direction in which you
are looking for happiness." ... Happiness can be found
only in the experience of union with God, the experience that also unites us to everyone else in the human
family and to all reality. This return to unity is the good
news that the liturgy proclaims. (*MC,* 5)

Isaiah 52:7 NASB

How lovely on the mountains
Are the feet of him who brings good news,
Who announces peace
And brings good news of happiness,
Who announces salvation....

· December 4 ·

Abba, Father

[Call God] "Father, dear Father."
Romans 8:15 NLT

The Liturgical Year . . . is a comprehensive program designed to enable the Christian people to assimilate the special graces attached to the principal events of Jesus' life. The divine plan according to Paul is to share with us the knowledge of the Father that belongs to the Word of God by nature and to the man Christ Jesus who was united to that Word. This consciousness is crystallized in Jesus' remarkable expression "Abba," translated "Father." "Abba" implies a relationship of awe, affection and intimacy. Jesus' personal experience of God as Abba is the heart of the Mystery that is being transmitted through the liturgy. The Liturgical Year provides the maximum communication of this consciousness. (*MC*, 5–6)

Romans 8:15 NASB

For you have not received a spirit of slavery leading to fear again, but you have received a spirit of adoption as sons [and daughters] by which we cry out, "Abba! Father!"

· *December 5* ·

The Liturgical Year
and the Body of Christ

Be mature and full grown in the Lord....
Ephesians 4:13 NLT

Each [liturgical] year...presents, relives and transmits
the entire scope of the Mystery of Christ. As the process continues year after year, like a tree adding new
rings to its growth, we grow toward maturity in Christ.
And the expansion of our individual faith experience
manifests the developing corporate personality of the
New Creation called by Paul the "Body of Christ." The
"Body of Christ," or simply "the Christ," is the symbol for Paul of the unfolding of the human family into
Christ-consciousness, that is, into Christ's experience of
the Ultimate Reality as *Abba*. Each of us, as living cells
in the body of Christ, contributes to this cosmic plan
through our own growth in faith and love and by sup-
porting the same growth in others. Hence, the immense
value of corporate worship and of sharing and celebrating the experience of the Mystery of Christ in a faith
community. (*MC*, 6)

Ephesians 4:16 NLT

As each part [of the body of Christ] does its own special
work, it helps the other parts grow, so that the whole
body is healthy and growing and full of love.

· December 6 ·

An Overview Followed by Close-ups

My soul is consumed with longing....
Psalm 119:20 NIV

Each [liturgical] season presents ... an overview ... while the particular feasts ... present close-ups of the action of Jesus in us and in the world. For example, the Christmas-Epiphany Mystery begins with the season of Advent, an extended period of preparation that culminates in the climactic feast of Christmas.... The first Sunday of Advent ... gives us a broad view of the three-fold coming of Christ. On the following Sundays we are introduced to the three central figures of Advent: Mary, the Virgin Mother of the Savior; John the Baptist, who introduced Jesus to those who first heard his message; and Isaiah, who prophesied Christ's coming with extraordinary accuracy.... These principals become living models for us to imitate. In this way, the liturgy awakens in us longings similar to those of the prophets who yearned for the coming of the Messiah. We are thus prepared for the spiritual birth of Jesus in us through our participation in the unfolding of the Christmas-Epiphany Mystery. (*MC*, 7–8)

Psalm 119:174 NIV

I long for your salvation, O LORD....

· December 7 ·

Celebrate the Mysteries of Christ

This mystery ... is Christ in you. ...
Colossians 1:27 NIV

The entire scope of the mystery of Christ is experienced at ever-deepening levels of assimilation as we celebrate the liturgical seasons. ... We are invited ... to relate to Christ on every level of his being as well as our own. This developing relationship with Christ is the main thrust of the liturgical seasons. ... The transmission of this personal relationship with Christ — and through him with the Father — is what Paul calls the *Mysterion*, the Greek word for mystery or sacrament, an external sign that contains and communicates sacred Reality. The liturgy teaches and empowers us, as we celebrate the mysteries of Christ, to perceive them not only as historical events, but as manifestations of Christ here and now. Through this living contact with Christ, we become icons of Christ, that is, manifestations of the Gospel in ... daily life. (*MC*, 8)

Colossians 1:27 NIV

God has chosen to make known among the Gentiles the glorious riches of this mystery, which is Christ in you, the hope of glory.

· *December 8* ·

Enhance Your Capacity
to Listen to the Word of God

Prepare the way of the LORD!
Isaiah 40:3 NAB

The consciousness of Christ is transmitted to us in the liturgy according to our preparation. The best preparation for receiving this transmission is the regular practice of contemplative prayer, which refines and enhances our capacity to listen and to respond to the word of God in scripture and in the liturgy. The desire to assimilate and to be assimilated into Christ's inner experience of the Ultimate Reality as Abba also characterizes contemplative prayer. The liturgy is God's way par excellence of transmitting Christ-consciousness. It is the chief place where it happens. It makes use of ritual to prepare the minds and hearts of the worshipers. When we are properly prepared, it grasps our attention at every level of our being and the special grace of the feast is, in fact, communicated. (*MC*, 8–9)

Ezekiel 3:10 NASB

Take into your heart all My words
which I will speak to you and listen closely.

· *December 9* ·

The Celebration of the Transmission of Divine Light

The unfolding of your words gives light....
Psalm 119:130 NIV

Each liturgical season has a period of preparation that readies us for the celebration of the climactic feast. The feast of Christmas is the first burst of light in the unfolding of the Christmas-Epiphany Mystery. Theologically, Christmas is the revelation of the Eternal Word made flesh. But it takes time to celebrate and penetrate all that this event actually contains and involves. The most we can do on Christmas night is gasp in wonderment and rejoice with the angels and the shepherds who first experienced it. The various aspects of the Mystery of divine light are examined one by one in the days following Christmas. The liturgy carefully unpacks the marvelous treasures that are contained in the initial burst of light. Actually, we do not grasp the full import of the Mystery until we move through the other two cycles [Easter-Ascension and Pentecost]. As the divine light grows brighter, it reveals what it contains, that is, divine life; and divine life reveals that the Ultimate Reality is love. (*MC*, 15–16)

Psalm 43:3 NIV

Send forth your light and your truth, let them guide me; let them bring me ... to the place where you dwell.

· December 10 ·

The Ripe Fruit of the Christmas-Epiphany Mystery

He is truly in me.
Thomas Merton

The coming of Christ into our conscious lives is the ripe fruit of the Christmas-Epiphany Mystery. It presupposes a presence of Christ that is already within us waiting to be awakened. This might be called the fourth coming of Christ, except that it is not a coming in the strict sense since it is already here. The Christmas-Epiphany Mystery invites us to take possession of what is already ours. As Thomas Merton put it, we are "to become what we already are." The Christmas-Epiphany Mystery, as the coming of Christ into our lives, makes us aware of the fact that he is already here as our true self — the deepest reality in us and in everyone else. Once God takes upon himself the human condition, everyone is potentially divine. Through the Incarnation of his Son, God floods the whole human family — past, present and to come — with his majesty, dignity and grace. Christ dwells in us in a mysterious but real way. (*MC*, 16–17)

Galatians 2:20 NAB

I live, no longer I, but Christ lives in me....

· December 11 ·

Advent Liturgy Includes John the Baptist

Are you really the Messiah?
Luke 7:19 TCLB

The light of Christmas grows in each of us as the Advent season progresses, manifesting itself through flashes of insight that bring intimations of the dazzling light of the Christmas-Epiphany Mystery.... John the Baptist had staked his integrity as a prophet on pointing to Jesus as the Messiah.... He began to have doubts about whether he had pointed out the right man.... Notice the agonizing double-bind.... Jesus was not acting as the Messiah was expected to act. Accordingly, John sent his disciples to Jesus to ask, "Are you the Messiah or do we look for another?" The question suggests the full extent of the problem of conscience that he was enduring. Should he now disclaim the one he had previously proclaimed to be the Messiah? That was his great doubt. He could not decide which course to follow. So he sent his disciples to question the very person upon whose identity he had staked his own prophetic mission — the one, to use his own words, "whose sandals I am not worthy to loose." (*MC*, 18, 20)

Luke 7:20 NAB

John the Baptist has sent us to you to ask, "Are you the one who is to come, or should we look for another?"

· *December 12* ·

John's Double-Bind Resolved

Consider it pure joy....
James 1:2 NIV

In the presence of John's disciples, Jesus worked a series of miracles that he knew would reassure John, fulfilling the prophesy of Isaiah which speaks of the blind receiving their sight and the poor having the Gospel preached to them. That was the resolution of John's double-bind. Why did John suffer so terrible a trial right at the end of his life? The double-bind is sometimes designed to free us from the last vestiges of cultural conditioning, including our religious cultural conditioning. The means that we needed in the early part of our spiritual journey (but which we may have come to depend on too much) are gradually removed. One of the classical ways of removing them is a double-bind that forces one to grow beyond the limitations of one's culture, the influences of early childhood and one's early religious background. (*MC*, 20)

Luke 7:23 NLT

And tell him, "God blesses those who are not offended by me."

· *December 13* ·

Freedom from Cultural Conditioning

What did you go out to see?
Luke 7:25 NIV

Family, ethnic and religious values are important and may support us for a certain time and to a certain place in the spiritual journey, but not to the place of total freedom that is God's ambition for each of us. Perhaps it was John's preconceived ideas about asceticism that God wanted to demolish in order to free him in the last days of his life to accept God's coming in any way at all, including through the eating and drinking and compassion of the actual Messiah. Jesus, by the miracles he worked in the presence of John's disciples, thus said to John in answer to his question, "My friend, you did not make a mistake. I am the Messiah. But the Messiah is not limited to your ideas of what he should do and how he should behave." That solved John's double-bind. (*MC*, 20–21)

Luke 7:22, 24–26, 34 NIV

Go back and report to John what you have seen and heard: The blind receive sight, the lame walk.... What did you go into the desert to see? A reed swayed by the wind?... A man dressed in fine clothes?... A prophet?... The Son of Man came eating and drinking ...a friend of tax collectors and "sinners."

· *December 14* ·

Advent Liturgy Includes Mary

I am the Lord's servant....
Luke 1:38 NIV

The experience of the double-bind hit Mary...at the age of fourteen or fifteen. She had set up a plan for her life according to what she firmly believed was God's will. Along comes the Angel Gabriel and says, "God wants you to be the mother of the Messiah." Mary was greatly troubled by the message of the angel. The underpinnings of her whole spiritual journey were shaken. She could not understand how God could have led her to believe that he wanted her to be a virgin and then be told by his messenger, "I want you to be a mother." (*MC*, 21)

Luke 1:38 NIV

"I am the Lord's servant," Mary answered. "May it be to me as you have said."

· December 15 ·

Angel's Response to Mary's Dilemma

Nothing is impossible with God.
Luke 1:37 NIV

"How is this to be since I do not know man?" was Mary's response. Notice the discretion of these words. She does not say she won't do it, but she delicately raises the problem of how it can be done since "I do not (and will not) know man." In other words, she takes her dilemma and respectfully places it in God's lap. "You created the problem," she seems to say, "Please solve it. I'm not saying yes. And, I'm not saying no. Please tell me how this problem is to be resolved." The angel then goes on to explain, "The Holy Spirit will overshadow you." Her motherhood, in other words, is going to be outside the normal course of procreation. She will be able to consent to it because God is creating something absolutely unheard-of in human experience: a Virgin Mother. (*MC*, 21)

Luke 1:34–35, 37 NIV

"How will this be," Mary asked the angel, "since I am a virgin?" The angel answered, "The Holy Spirit will come upon you, and the power of the Most High will overshadow you. So the holy one to be born will be called the Son of God.... For nothing is impossible with God."

· *December 16* ·

News from the Angel Gabriel

God, who calls you, is faithful. . . .
1 Thessalonians 5:24 NLT

The news the angel brought and its consequences completely disrupted Mary's plans for her life. Her mother soon became aware of her mysterious pregnancy. Joseph was so upset over it that he thought about giving her up. In other words, this pregnancy turned her life upside-down. Instead of being a respectable young woman engaged to Joseph, she now appeared to be someone who had engaged in premarital relations. She became one of the many disreputable people in her disreputable town. The same God who had inspired her to choose a celibate life made her the mother of the Messiah. (*MC,* 21–22)

Luke 1:31 NIV

You will be with child and give birth to a son, and you are to give him the name Jesus. He will be great and will be called the Son of the Most High.

· December 17 ·

Open Ourselves to a
Higher State of Consciousness

I was blind but now I see!
John 9:25 NIV

As human beings, we cannot presume that God will do something that has never been done before.... But we can be sure of that if we allow the creative energies of the double-bind to do their work, at some moment we will find ourselves in a higher state of consciousness. Suddenly we will perceive a new way of seeing all reality. Our old world view will end. A new relationship with God, ourselves and other people will emerge based on the new level of understanding, perception and union with God we have been given. The double-bind frees us to grow into an expanded relationship with all reality beginning with God. During Advent, as we celebrate the renewed coming of divine light, we receive encouragement to open to God's coming in any way that he may choose. This is the disposition that opens us completely to the light. (*MC*, 22)

Isaiah 9:2 NRSV

The people who walked in darkness have seen a great light; those who lived in a land of deep darkness — on them light has shined.

· *December 18* ·

Ongoing Purification

The LORD tests the heart.
Proverbs 17:3 NIV

We observed that Mary, after questioning the angel carefully, surmounted her double-bind by a leap of confidence. Her dilemma was resolved in an absolutely unexpected way by her becoming simultaneously Virgin and Mother, demonstrating that there is no double-bind impossible for God to resolve. Even John the Baptist and Mary could not escape from God's enthusiasm to make them holier still. Difficulties give God the opportunity to refine and purify our motivation. They give us an opportunity to make a greater surrender. (*MC*, 22)

Job 23:10 NKJV

When He has tested me, I shall come forth as gold.

· *December 19* ·

Live a Life of Love

Live a life of love....
Ephesians 5:2 *NIV*

What is Mary's first response to the gift of divine motherhood? She goes to see her cousin Elizabeth who
happens to be having a baby and who needs help with
whatever you do when you are getting ready for a baby:
making diapers, preparing the bassinet, knitting little
socks and bonnets. That is what she figured God wanted
her to do. It never occurred to her to tell anyone about
her incredible privilege. She simply did what she ordinarily did: she went to serve somebody in need. That is
what the divine action is always suggesting: help someone at hand in some small but practical way. As you
learn to love more, you can help more. (*MC*, 24)

Ephesians 5:1–2 *NIV*

Be imitators of God, therefore, as dearly loved children
and live a life of love, just as Christ loved us and gave
himself up for us as a fragrant offering and sacrifice
to God.

· December 20 ·

Doing What We Are Supposed to Be Doing

Give, and it will be given to you.
Luke 6:38 NIV

Mary entered the house of Elizabeth and said hello. The Presence that she carried within her was transmitted to Elizabeth by the sound of her voice. In response, the baby in Elizabeth's womb leapt for joy; he was sanctified by Mary's simple greeting. God's greatest works take place without our doing anything spectacular. They are almost side-effects of doing the ordinary things we are supposed to be doing. If you are transformed, everybody in your life will be changed too. There is a sense in which we create the world in which we live. If you are pouring out love everywhere you go, that love will start coming back; it cannot be otherwise. The more you give, the more you will receive. (*MC*, 24)

Luke 1:41 NJB

Now it happened that as soon as Elizabeth heard Mary's greeting, the child leapt in her womb and Elizabeth was filled with the Holy Spirit.

· *December 21* ·

Fulfill the Duties of Our Job in Life

Fulfill the duties imposed on us....
Jean-Pierre de Caussade

Following Mary's example, the fundamental practice for healing the wounds of the false-self system is to fulfill the duties of our job in life. This includes helping people who are counting on us. If prayer gets in the way, there is some misunderstanding. Some devout persons think that if their activities at home or their job get in the way of praying, there is something wrong with their activities. On the contrary, there is something wrong with their prayer. (*MC*, 24)

Psalm 37:3 NRSV

Trust in the LORD, and do good....

· December 22 ·

Ordinary Actions Can Transmit
Divine Love

All of us ... are being transformed. ...
2 Corinthians 3:18 NRSV

Contemplative prayer enables us to see the treasures of
sanctification and the opportunities for spiritual growth
that are present day by day in ordinary life. If one is
transformed, one can walk down the street, drink a cup
of tea or shake hands with somebody and be pouring
divine life into the world. In Christianity motivation is
everything. When the love of Christ is the principal motivation, ordinary actions transmit divine love. This is
the fundamental Christian witness; this is evangelization
in its primary form. (*MC*, 24–25)

Ephesians 4:23–24 NAB

Be renewed in the spirit of your minds, and put on
the new self, created in God's way in righteousness and
holiness of truth.

· *December 23* ·

Awakening in Others Their Divine Potential

Won without a word....
1 Peter 3:1 NASB

A sanctified person is like a radio or TV station sending
out signals. Whoever has the proper receptive apparatus can receive the transmission. What Mary teaches us
by her visit to Elizabeth is that the sound of her voice
awakened the transcendent potential in another person
without her saying anything. She was simply Mary, the
ark of the Covenant; that is, one in whom God was
dwelling. Thus, when Mary said hello to Elizabeth, the
child in her womb leapt for joy. His divine potentiality
was fully awakened. So was Elizabeth's. She was filled
with the Holy Spirit. This is the most sublime kind of
communication. Transmission is not preaching as such.
Transmission is the capacity to awaken in other people
their own potentiality to become divine. (*MC, 25*)

1 Peter 3:1-2 NIV

That...they may be won over without words...when
they see the purity and reverence of your lives.

· *December 24* ·

Joy of Christmas

Shout with joy to God, all the earth!
Psalm 66:1 NIV

The joy of Christmas is the intuition that all limitations to growth into higher states of consciousness have been overcome. The divine light cuts across all darkness, prejudice, preconceived ideas, prepackaged values, false expectations, phoniness and hypocrisy. It presents us with the truth. To act out of the truth is to make Christ grow not only in ourselves, but in others. Thus, the humdrum duties and events of daily life become sacramental, shot through with eternal implications. This is what we celebrate in the liturgy. The *kairos*, "the appointed time," is *now*. According to Paul, "Now is the time of salvation," that is, now is the time when the whole of the divine mercy is available. Now is the time to risk further growth. (*MC*, 27)

2 Corinthian 6:2 NIV

I tell you, now is the time of God's favor,
now is the day of salvation.

· December 25 ·

Light of Christmas

Glory to God in the highest....
Luke 2:14 NAB

Readiness for any eventuality is the attitude of one who has entered into the freedom of the Gospel. Commitment to the new world that Christ is creating . . . requires flexibility and detachment: the readiness to go anywhere or nowhere, to live or to die, to rest or to work, to be sick or to be well, to take up one service and to put down another. Everything is important when one is opening to Christ-consciousness. This awareness transforms our worldly concepts of security into the security of accepting, for love of God, an unknown future.... The light of Christmas is an explosion of insight changing our whole idea of God. Our childish ways of thinking of God are left behind. As we turn our enchanted gaze toward the Babe in the crib, our inmost being opens to the new consciousness that the Babe has brought into the world. (*MC*, 28)

Luke 2:11 NIV

Today in the town of David a Savior has been born to you; he is Christ the Lord.

· December 26 ·

Manifestation of Jesus in His Divinity

Let your light shine for all ... to see.
Isaiah 60:1 NLT

The manifestation of Jesus in his divinity to the Gentiles in the persons of the Magi [Matthew 2:9–12] is supplemented by two other events that are manifestations of Jesus' divine nature from a later period in his life.... The second text recalls the manifestation of Jesus in his divinity to the Jews at the river Jordan [Mark 1:9–11].... The third text recalls the manifestation of Jesus in his divine Person to his disciples at the wedding feast of Cana [John 2:1–12].... These three readings are an integral part of the celebration of Epiphany, the crowning feast of the Christmas-Epiphany Mystery and the full revelation of all that the light of Christmas contains.... The liturgy is primarily a parable of what grace is doing now; it disregards historical considerations and juxtaposes texts in order to bring out the sublime significance of what is being transmitted in an invisible way through the visible signs. (*MC*, 28–29)

Isaiah 60:1 NLT

Arise, Jerusalem! Let your light shine for all the nations to see! For the glory of the LORD is shining upon you.

· *December 27* ·

Jesus' Baptism in the Jordan

This is my Son, whom I love.
Matthew 3:17 NIV

Jesus' Baptism in the Jordan and the Marriage Feast of Cana are integrated into the celebration in order to enlarge the perspective from which we perceive the divinity of Jesus. Jesus' baptism by John represents the manifestation of Jesus' divinity to the Jews, the moment when Jesus entered fully into his mission for the salvation of the human family. His baptism in the Jordan is a preview of the graces of Easter and Pentecost, in which we celebrate the Mysteries of divine life and love. Jesus' descent into the waters of the Jordan anticipates his descent into the sufferings of his passion and death; his emergence from the Jordan symbolizes his resurrection; and the Dove's descent prefigures the outpouring of the Holy Spirit at Pentecost. (*MC*, 29–30)

Matthew 3:17 NIV

And a voice from heaven said, "This is my Son, whom I love; with him I am well pleased."

· *December 28* ·

Significance of the Marriage Feast of Cana

He ... revealed his glory. ...
John 2:11 NIV

Epiphany, as the celebration of the marriage of the Son of God with human nature, reveals the deepest significance of the Eternal Word becoming a human being. Furthermore, it is our personal call not only to the surrender of faith, but to transformation into divine life and love. The marriage feast [of Cana], taking place in a tiny out-of-the-way town, becomes the symbol of the most fantastic event in human history, the most striking example of how eternal time enters into chronological time and transforms it. What happens when the wine begins to run out and the bridal couple are in danger of embarrassment, becomes a cosmic event. What Jesus does at the marriage feast is the symbol of what he will later accomplish through his passion, death and resurrection. (*MC*, 31–32)

John 2:11 NIV

This, the first of his miraculous signs, Jesus performed at Cana in Galilee. He thus revealed his glory, and his disciples put their faith in him.

· *December 29* ·

Special Grace of Epiphany

All of you . . . are Christ's body. . . .
1 Corinthians 12:27 NLT

Epiphany is the crowning feast of Christmas. We tend to think of Christmas as the greater feast, but in actual fact, it is only the beginning. It whets our appetite for the treasures to be revealed in the feasts to come. The great enlightenment of the Christmas-Epiphany Mystery is when we perceive that the divine light manifests not only that the Son of God has become a human being, but that we are incorporated as living members into his body. This is the special grace of Epiphany. (*MC*, 16)

1 Corinthians 12:27 NLT

Now all of you together are Christ's body, and each one of you is a separate and necessary part of it.

· *December 30* ·

The Fullness of Christ

[Attain to]...the fullness of Christ....
Ephesians 4:13 NIV

As living cells in the Body of Christ, we are caught up in the process that is moving toward the *pleroma*. This term describes the ripening development of Christ-consciousness shared by each of the individual cells in the corporate Body of Christ.... We can cling to the old Adam and solidarity with him, or we can accept the Spirit inviting us to unlimited personal and corporate growth in Christ, the new Adam. (*MC*, 32–33)

Ephesians 4:13 NIV

Become mature, attaining to the whole measure of the fullness of Christ.

· December 31 ·

An Invitation to Become Divine

Open the door [and] I will come in.…
Revelation 3:20 NLT

In view of his divine dignity and power, the Son of God gathers into himself the entire human family past, present and future. The moment that the Eternal Word is uttered outside the bosom of the Trinity and steps forth into the human condition, the Word gives himself to all creatures.… The meaning of the life and message of Jesus is that the reign of God is "close at hand": the whole of God is now available for every human being who wants him. Epiphany, then, is the manifestation of all that is contained in the light of Christmas; it is the invitation to become divine. (*MC*, 16)

Revelation 3:20 NLT

Here I stand at the door and knock. If you hear me calling and open the door, I will come in, and we will share a meal as friends.

Appendix

The Method of Centering Prayer:
The Prayer of Consent

By Thomas Keating

"Be still and know that I am God."
Psalm 46:10

Contemplative Prayer

We may think of prayer as thoughts or feelings expressed in words. But this is only one expression. In the Christian tradition Contemplative Prayer is considered to be the pure gift of God. It is the opening of mind and heart — our whole being — to God, the Ultimate Mystery, beyond thoughts, words, and emotions. Through grace we open our awareness to God whom we know by faith is within us, closer than breathing, closer than thinking, closer than choosing — closer than consciousness itself.

Centering Prayer

Centering Prayer is a method designed to facilitate the development of Contemplative Prayer by preparing our faculties to receive this gift. It is an attempt to present the teaching of earlier times in an updated form. Centering Prayer is not meant to replace other kinds of prayer; rather, it casts a new light and depth of meaning on them. It is at the same time a relationship with God and a discipline to foster that relationship. This method of prayer is a movement beyond conversation with Christ to communion with Him.

Theological Background

The source of Centering Prayer, as in all methods leading to Contemplative Prayer, is the indwelling Trinity: Father, Son, and Holy Spirit. The focus of Centering Prayer is the deepening of our relationship with the living Christ. It tends to build communities of faith and bond the members together in mutual friendship and love.

The Root of Centering Prayer

Listening to the word of God in Scripture (Lectio Divina) is a traditional way of cultivating friendship with Christ. It is a way of listening to the texts of Scripture as if we were in conversation with Christ and He were suggesting the topics of conversation. The daily encounter with Christ and reflection on His word leads beyond mere acquaintanceship to an attitude of friendship, trust, and love. Conversation simplifies and gives way to communing. Gregory the Great (sixth century) in summarizing the Christian contemplative tradition expressed it as "resting in God." This was the classical meaning of Contemplative Prayer in the Christian tradition for the first sixteen centuries.

Wisdom Saying of Jesus

Centering Prayer is based on the wisdom saying of Jesus in the Sermon on the Mount:

> "... But when you pray, go to your inner room,
> close the door and pray to your Father in secret.
> And your Father, who sees in secret, will reward you."
> Matthew 6:6

It is also inspired by writings of major contributors to the Christian contemplative heritage including John Cassian, the anonymous author of *The Cloud of Unknowing*, Francis de Sales, Teresa of Avila, John of the Cross, Thérèse of Lisieux, and Thomas Merton.

Centering Prayer Guidelines

1. Choose a sacred word as the symbol of your intention to consent to God's presence and action within.
2. Sitting comfortably and with eyes closed, settle briefly and silently introduce the sacred word as the symbol of your consent to God's presence and action within.
3. When engaged with your thoughts,* return ever-so-gently to the sacred word.
4. At the end of the prayer period, remain in silence with eyes closed for a couple of minutes.

---

*Thoughts include body sensations, feelings, images, and reflections.

Explanation of the Guidelines

I. **Choose a sacred word as the symbol of your intention to consent to God's presence and action within (see Thomas Keating, *Open Mind, Open Heart*, chapter 5).**

1. The sacred word expresses our intention to consent to God's presence and action within.

2. The sacred word is chosen during a brief period of prayer asking the Holy Spirit to inspire us with one that is especially suitable for us.

a. Examples: God, Jesus, Abba, Father, Mother, Mary, Amen.

b. Other possibilities: Love, Listen, Peace, Mercy, Let Go, Silence, Stillness, Faith, Trust.

3. Instead of a sacred word, a simple inward glance toward the Divine Presence, or noticing one's breath, may be more suitable for some persons. The same guidelines apply to these symbols as to the sacred word.

4. The sacred word is sacred not because of its inherent meaning, but because of the meaning we give it as the expression of our intention and consent.

5. Having chosen a sacred word, we do not change it during the prayer period because that would be to start thinking again.

II. **Sitting comfortably and with eyes closed, settle briefly and silently introduce the sacred word as the symbol of your consent to God's presence and action within.**

1. "Sitting comfortably" means relatively comfortably so as not to encourage sleep during the time of prayer.

2. Whatever sitting position we choose, we keep the back straight.

3. We close our eyes as a symbol of letting go of what is going on around and within us.

4. We introduce the sacred word inwardly as gently as laying a feather on a piece of absorbent cotton.

5. Should we fall asleep, upon awakening, we continue the prayer.

III. When engaged with your thoughts, return ever-so-gently to the sacred word.

1. "Thoughts" is an umbrella term for every perception, including body sensations, sense perceptions, feelings, images, memories, plans, reflections, concepts, commentaries, and spiritual experiences.
2. Thoughts are an inevitable, integral, and normal part of Centering Prayer.
3. By "returning ever-so-gently to the sacred word" a minimum of effort is indicated. This is the only activity we initiate during the time of Centering Prayer.
4. During the course of Centering Prayer, the sacred word may become vague or disappear.

IV. At the end of the prayer period, remain in silence with eyes closed for a couple of minutes.

1. The additional two minutes enables us to bring the atmosphere of silence into everyday life.
2. If this prayer is done in a group, the leader may slowly recite a prayer such as the Lord's Prayer, while the others listen.

Some Practical Points

1. The minimum time for this prayer is twenty minutes. Two periods are recommended each day, one first thing in the morning and the other in the afternoon or early evening. With practice the time may be extended to thirty minutes or longer.
2. The end of the prayer period can be indicated by a timer which does not have an audible tick or loud sound when it goes off.
3. Possible physical symptoms during the prayer:
   a. We may notice slight pains, itches, or twitches in various parts of the body or a generalized sense of restlessness. These are usually due to the untying of emotional knots in the body.
   b. We may notice heaviness or lightness in our extremities. This is usually due to a deep level of spiritual attentiveness.
   c. In all cases we pay no attention and ever-so-gently return to the sacred word.

4. The principal fruits of the prayer are experienced in daily life and not during the prayer period.

5. Centering Prayer familiarizes us with God's first language, which is silence.

Points for Further Development

1. During the prayer period, various kinds of thoughts may arise:

    a. Ordinary wanderings of the imagination or memory.
    b. Thoughts and feelings that give rise to attractions or aversions.
    c. Insights and psychological breakthroughs.
    d. Self-reflections such as, "How am I doing?" or, "This peace is just great!"
    e. Thoughts and feelings that arise from the unloading of the unconscious.
    f. When engaged with any of these thoughts return ever-so-gently to the sacred word.

2. During this prayer we avoid analyzing our experience, harboring expectations, or aiming at some specific goal such as:

    a. Repeating the sacred word continuously.
    b. Having no thoughts.
    c. Making the mind a blank.
    d. Feeling peaceful or consoled.
    e. Achieving a spiritual experience (see *Open Mind, Open Heart*, chapters 6–10).

Ways to Deepen Our Relationship with God

1. Practice two twenty-to-thirty-minute periods of Centering Prayer daily.

2. Listen to the Word of God in Scripture and study *Open Mind, Open Heart*.

3. Select one or two of the specific practices for everyday life as suggested in *Open Mind, Open Heart*, chapter 12.

4. Join a weekly Centering Prayer Group.

    a. It encourages the members of the group to persevere in their individual practices.

b. It provides an opportunity for further input on a regular basis through tapes, readings, and discussion.
c. It offers an opportunity to support and share the spiritual journey.

What Centering Prayer Is and Is Not

1. It is not a technique but a way of cultivating a deeper relationship with God.
2. It is not a relaxation exercise but it may be quite refreshing.
3. It is not a form of self-hypnosis but a way to quiet the mind while maintaining its alertness.
4. It is not a charismatic gift but a path of transformation.
5. It is not a para-psychological experience but an exercise of faith, hope, and selfless love.
6. It is not limited to the "felt" presence of God but is rather a deepening of faith in God's abiding presence.
7. It is not reflective or spontaneous prayer but simply resting in God beyond thoughts, words, and emotions.

For information and resources contact:

Contemplative Outreach, Ltd.
10 Park Place — P.O. Box 737
Butler, NJ 07405
Tel: (973) 838-3384 / Fax: (973) 492-5795
Email: *office@coutreach.org*

Visit our website at
www.contemplativeoutreach.org
for events, retreats, articles, and the on-line bookstore.

Reprinted with permission
© 2005 Contemplative Outreach, Ltd.

Index of Biblical References

Key to Scripture Citations

KJV	King James Version
NAB	New American Bible
NASB	New American Standard Bible
NIV	New International Version
NJB	New Jerusalem Bible
NKJV	New King James Version
NLT	New Living Translation
NRSV	New Revised Standard Version
TCLB	The Catholic Living Bible
THS	The Holy Scriptures

Index of Subjects

Index of Quotations

JANUARY 6: Fourteenth-century author, "A short prayer pierces the heavens." *The Cloud of Unknowing*, ed. William Johnston (New York: Image Books/Doubleday, 1973), 96.

JANUARY 15: Soul of Christ, sanctify me. *Anima Christi*.

JANUARY 16: Closer my God to Thee. *Traditional Hymn*.

JANUARY 25: Body of Christ, save me. *Anima Christi*.

FEBRUARY 7: Saint Teresa of Avila, "Love turns work into rest." *The Collected Works of Saint Teresa*, 2d ed., vol. 1. Translated by Kieran Kavanaugh, O.C.D., and Otilio Rodriguez, O.C.D. (Washington, D.C.: ICS Publications, Institute of Carmelite Studies, 1987), 448.

FEBRUARY 22: Evagrius, "[Pray]...in ardent love for God...." *De Oratione*, n. 61, quoted in Thomas Merton, *Contemplative Prayer* (New York: Image Books, Doubleday, 1996), 48.

FEBRUARY 26: Abba Isaac, "[Here's]...a formula of salvation...." *John Cassian, Conferences*, translation and preface by Colm Luibheid (New York: Paulist Press, 1985), 135.

FEBRUARY 28: Go in peace to love and serve the world. *Dismissal from Mass*.

MARCH 12: Cardinal Newman, "Jesus, help me to spread your fragrance...." Cardinal Newman Prayer, quoted in *Mother Teresa: In Her Own Words*, compiled by Jose Luis Gonzalez-Balado (New York: Gramercy Books, Random House Value Publishing, 1997 edition), 10.

MARCH 22: Saint John of the Cross, "O living flame of love...." The Living Flame of Love, stanza 1, *The Collected Works of St. John of the Cross*, translated by Kieran Kavanaugh, O.C.D., and Otilio Rodriguez, O.C.D. (Washington, D.C.: ICS Publications, Institute of Carmelite Studies, 1991), 52.

MARCH 23: The power of this night dispels all evil, washes guilt away, and restores lost innocence.... *Exultet, Paschal Vigil*.

Index of Original
Active Prayer Sentences

Permissions

Acknowledgment is gratefully made to the following publishers for permission to reprint excerpts:

CISTERCIAN PUBLICATIONS, Western Michigan United Station, Kalamazoo, MI 49008, for an excerpt from *Contemplative Prayer* by Thomas Merton, originally published as *The Climate of Monastic Prayer* by Cistercian Publications, © 1969 by The Merton Legacy Trust. Used by permission.

CURTIS BROWN LTD., Ten Astor Place, New York, NY 10003, for an excerpt from *The Sign of Jonas* by Thomas Merton, © 1953 by the Abbey of Our Lady of Gethsemani. Copyright renewed 1981 by The Trustees of the Merton Legacy Trust. Used by permission of Curtis Brown Ltd. for the British Commonwealth.

THE CONTINUUM INTERNATIONAL PUBLISHING GROUP, INC., 370 Lexington Avenue, New York, NY 10017 for excerpts from *Psalms for Praying: An Invitation to Wholeness* by Nan C. Merrill, © 1996 by Nan C. Merrill; *The Mystery of Christ: The Liturgy as Spiritual Experience* by Thomas Keating, © 1987 by St. Benedict's Monastery; *Open Mind, Open Heart: The Contemplative Dimension of the Gospel* by Thomas Keating, © 1986, 1992 by St. Benedict's Monastery; *The Better Part: Stages of Contemplative Living* by Thomas Keating, © 2000 by St. Benedict's Monastery, Snowmass, Colorado; *Crisis of Faith, Crisis of Love* by Thomas Keating, 3rd revised edition © 1995 by St. Benedict's Monastery, Snowmass, Colorado; *Invitation to Love: The Way of Christian Contemplation* by Thomas Keating, © 1992 by St. Benedict's Monastery. Used by permission.

THE CROSSROAD PUBLISHING COMPANY, 481 Eighth Avenue, New York, NY 10001 for excerpts from *Awakenings* by Thomas Keating, © 1990 by St. Benedict's Abbey, Snowmass, Colorado; *The Heart of the World: An Introduction to Contemplative Christianity* by Thomas Keating as told to John Osborne © 1981, 1999 by

Bible Acknowledgments

Scripture quotations marked KJV are taken from the King James Version of the Bible. The King James Version of the Bible is in the public domain. No permission necessary.

Scripture texts marked NAB in this work are taken from the New American Bible with Revised New Testament and Revised Psalms © 1991, 1986, 1970 Confraternity of Christian Doctrine, Inc., Washington, D.C., and are used by permission of the copyright owner. All Rights Reserved. No part of the New American Bible may be reproduced in any form without permission in writing from the copyright owner.

Scripture marked NASB taken from the New American Standard Bible®, Copyright © 1960, 1962, 1963, 1968, 1971, 1972, 1973, 1975, 1977, 1995 by the Lockman Foundation. Used by permission.

Scripture marked NIV taken from the Holy Bible, New International Version. Copyright © 1973, 1978, 1984 by International Bible Society. Used by permission of Zondervan Publishing House.

Scripture quotations marked NJB are from the New Jerusalem Bible, copyright © 1985 by Darton, Longman & Todd, Ltd. and Doubleday, a division of Random House, Inc. Reprinted by Permission.

Scripture quotations marked NKJV are taken from the New King James Version. Copyright © 1982 by Thomas Nelson, Inc. Used by permission. All rights reserved.

Scripture quotations marked NLT are from the Holy Bible, New Living Translation, copyright © 1996. Used by permission of Tyndale House Publishers, Inc., Wheaton, IL 60189. All rights reserved.